C-1439   CAREER EXAMINATION SERIES

This is your
PASSBOOK for...

Programmer/ Programmer Analyst

Test Preparation Study Guide
Questions & Answers

NATIONAL LEARNING CORPORATION®

COPYRIGHT NOTICE

This book is SOLELY intended for, is sold ONLY to, and its use is RESTRICTED to individual, bona fide applicants or candidates who qualify by virtue of having seriously filed applications for appropriate license, certificate, professional and/or promotional advancement, higher school matriculation, scholarship, or other legitimate requirements of education and/or governmental authorities.

This book is NOT intended for use, class instruction, tutoring, training, duplication, copying, reprinting, excerption, or adaptation, etc., by:

1) Other publishers
2) Proprietors and/or Instructors of "Coaching" and/or Preparatory Courses
3) Personnel and/or Training Divisions of commercial, industrial, and governmental organizations
4) Schools, colleges, or universities and/or their departments and staffs, including teachers and other personnel
5) Testing Agencies or Bureaus
6) Study groups which seek by the purchase of a single volume to copy and/or duplicate and/or adapt this material for use by the group as a whole without having purchased individual volumes for each of the members of the group
7) Et al.

Such persons would be in violation of appropriate Federal and State statutes.

PROVISION OF LICENSING AGREEMENTS – Recognized educational, commercial, industrial, and governmental institutions and organizations, and others legitimately engaged in educational pursuits, including training, testing, and measurement activities, may address request for a licensing agreement to the copyright owners, who will determine whether, and under what conditions, including fees and charges, the materials in this book may be used them. In other words, a licensing facility exists for the legitimate use of the material in this book on other than an individual basis. However, it is asseverated and affirmed here that the material in this book CANNOT be used without the receipt of the express permission of such a licensing agreement from the Publishers. Inquiries re licensing should be addressed to the company, attention rights and permissions department.

All rights reserved, including the right of reproduction in whole or in part, in any form or by any means, electronic or mechanical, including photocopying, recording, or by any information storage and retrieval system, without permission in writing from the Publisher.

Copyright © 2025 by
National Learning Corporation

212 Michael Drive, Syosset, NY 11791
(516) 921-8888 • www.passbooks.com
E-mail: info@passbooks.com

PASSBOOK® SERIES

THE *PASSBOOK® SERIES* has been created to prepare applicants and candidates for the ultimate academic battlefield – the examination room.

At some time in our lives, each and every one of us may be required to take an examination – for validation, matriculation, admission, qualification, registration, certification, or licensure.

Based on the assumption that every applicant or candidate has met the basic formal educational standards, has taken the required number of courses, and read the necessary texts, the *PASSBOOK® SERIES* furnishes the one special preparation which may assure passing with confidence, instead of failing with insecurity. Examination questions – together with answers – are furnished as the basic vehicle for study so that the mysteries of the examination and its compounding difficulties may be eliminated or diminished by a sure method.

This book is meant to help you pass your examination provided that you qualify and are serious in your objective.

The entire field is reviewed through the huge store of content information which is succinctly presented through a provocative and challenging approach – the question-and-answer method.

A climate of success is established by furnishing the correct answers at the end of each test.

You soon learn to recognize types of questions, forms of questions, and patterns of questioning. You may even begin to anticipate expected outcomes.

You perceive that many questions are repeated or adapted so that you can gain acute insights, which may enable you to score many sure points.

You learn how to confront new questions, or types of questions, and to attack them confidently and work out the correct answers.

You note objectives and emphases, and recognize pitfalls and dangers, so that you may make positive educational adjustments.

Moreover, you are kept fully informed in relation to new concepts, methods, practices, and directions in the field.

You discover that you are actually taking the examination all the time: you are preparing for the examination by "taking" an examination, not by reading extraneous and/or supererogatory textbooks.

In short, this PASSBOOK®, used directedly, should be an important factor in helping you to pass your test.

PROGRAMMER/PROGRAMMER ANALYST

DUTIES
An employee in this class performs technical work in the development of computer programs and/or the design, implementation, enhancement and maintenance of software systems. Assists in preparation, review and analysis of detailed computer systems specifications. Prepares charts, tables and diagrams to assist in analyzing problems. Codes programs instructions; assists in writing procedure manuals; documents computer systems and programs. Performs related work as required.

SCOPE OF THE EXAMINATION
The written test will be designed to test for knowledge, skills, and/or abilities in such areas as:
1. Data processing concepts and terminology;
2. Programming techniques and concepts;
3. Systems analysis;
4. Symbolic logic; and
5. Preparing written material.

HOW TO TAKE A TEST

I. YOU MUST PASS AN EXAMINATION

A. WHAT EVERY CANDIDATE SHOULD KNOW

Examination applicants often ask us for help in preparing for the written test. What can I study in advance? What kinds of questions will be asked? How will the test be given? How will the papers be graded?

As an applicant for a civil service examination, you may be wondering about some of these things. Our purpose here is to suggest effective methods of advance study and to describe civil service examinations.

Your chances for success on this examination can be increased if you know how to prepare. Those "pre-examination jitters" can be reduced if you know what to expect. You can even experience an adventure in good citizenship if you know why civil service exams are given.

B. WHY ARE CIVIL SERVICE EXAMINATIONS GIVEN?

Civil service examinations are important to you in two ways. As a citizen, you want public jobs filled by employees who know how to do their work. As a job seeker, you want a fair chance to compete for that job on an equal footing with other candidates. The best-known means of accomplishing this two-fold goal is the competitive examination.

Exams are widely publicized throughout the nation. They may be administered for jobs in federal, state, city, municipal, town or village governments or agencies.

Any citizen may apply, with some limitations, such as the age or residence of applicants. Your experience and education may be reviewed to see whether you meet the requirements for the particular examination. When these requirements exist, they are reasonable and applied consistently to all applicants. Thus, a competitive examination may cause you some uneasiness now, but it is your privilege and safeguard.

C. HOW ARE CIVIL SERVICE EXAMS DEVELOPED?

Examinations are carefully written by trained technicians who are specialists in the field known as "psychological measurement," in consultation with recognized authorities in the field of work that the test will cover. These experts recommend the subject matter areas or skills to be tested; only those knowledges or skills important to your success on the job are included. The most reliable books and source materials available are used as references. Together, the experts and technicians judge the difficulty level of the questions.

Test technicians know how to phrase questions so that the problem is clearly stated. Their ethics do not permit "trick" or "catch" questions. Questions may have been tried out on sample groups, or subjected to statistical analysis, to determine their usefulness.

Written tests are often used in combination with performance tests, ratings of training and experience, and oral interviews. All of these measures combine to form the best-known means of finding the right person for the right job.

II. HOW TO PASS THE WRITTEN TEST

A. NATURE OF THE EXAMINATION

To prepare intelligently for civil service examinations, you should know how they differ from school examinations you have taken. In school you were assigned certain definite pages to read or subjects to cover. The examination questions were quite detailed and usually emphasized memory. Civil service exams, on the other hand, try to discover your present ability to perform the duties of a position, plus your potentiality to learn these duties. In other words, a civil service exam attempts to predict how successful you will be. Questions cover such a broad area that they cannot be as minute and detailed as school exam questions.

In the public service similar kinds of work, or positions, are grouped together in one "class." This process is known as *position-classification*. All the positions in a class are paid according to the salary range for that class. One class title covers all of these positions, and they are all tested by the same examination.

B. FOUR BASIC STEPS

1) Study the announcement

How, then, can you know what subjects to study? Our best answer is: "Learn as much as possible about the class of positions for which you've applied." The exam will test the knowledge, skills and abilities needed to do the work.

Your most valuable source of information about the position you want is the official exam announcement. This announcement lists the training and experience qualifications. Check these standards and apply only if you come reasonably close to meeting them.

The brief description of the position in the examination announcement offers some clues to the subjects which will be tested. Think about the job itself. Review the duties in your mind. Can you perform them, or are there some in which you are rusty? Fill in the blank spots in your preparation.

Many jurisdictions preview the written test in the exam announcement by including a section called "Knowledge and Abilities Required," "Scope of the Examination," or some similar heading. Here you will find out specifically what fields will be tested.

2) Review your own background

Once you learn in general what the position is all about, and what you need to know to do the work, ask yourself which subjects you already know fairly well and which need improvement. You may wonder whether to concentrate on improving your strong areas or on building some background in your fields of weakness. When the announcement has specified "some knowledge" or "considerable knowledge," or has used adjectives like "beginning principles of..." or "advanced ... methods," you can get a clue as to the number and difficulty of questions to be asked in any given field. More questions, and hence broader coverage, would be included for those subjects which are more important in the work. Now weigh your strengths and weaknesses against the job requirements and prepare accordingly.

3) Determine the level of the position

Another way to tell how intensively you should prepare is to understand the level of the job for which you are applying. Is it the entering level? In other words, is this the position in which beginners in a field of work are hired? Or is it an intermediate or advanced level? Sometimes this is indicated by such words as "Junior" or "Senior" in the class title. Other jurisdictions use Roman numerals to designate the level – Clerk I, Clerk II, for example. The word "Supervisor" sometimes appears in the title. If the level is not indicated by the title, check the description of duties. Will you be working under very close supervision, or will you have responsibility for independent decisions in this work?

4) Choose appropriate study materials

Now that you know the subjects to be examined and the relative amount of each subject to be covered, you can choose suitable study materials. For beginning level jobs, or even advanced ones, if you have a pronounced weakness in some aspect of your training, read a modern, standard textbook in that field. Be sure it is up to date and has general coverage. Such books are normally available at your library, and the librarian will be glad to help you locate one. For entry-level positions, questions of appropriate difficulty are chosen – neither highly advanced questions, nor those too simple. Such questions require careful thought but not advanced training.

If the position for which you are applying is technical or advanced, you will read more advanced, specialized material. If you are already familiar with the basic principles of your field, elementary textbooks would waste your time. Concentrate on advanced textbooks and technical periodicals. Think through the concepts and review difficult problems in your field.

These are all general sources. You can get more ideas on your own initiative, following these leads. For example, training manuals and publications of the government agency which employs workers in your field can be useful, particularly for technical and professional positions. A letter or visit to the government department involved may result in more specific study suggestions, and certainly will provide you with a more definite idea of the exact nature of the position you are seeking.

III. KINDS OF TESTS

Tests are used for purposes other than measuring knowledge and ability to perform specified duties. For some positions, it is equally important to test ability to make adjustments to new situations or to profit from training. In others, basic mental abilities not dependent on information are essential. Questions which test these things may not appear as pertinent to the duties of the position as those which test for knowledge and information. Yet they are often highly important parts of a fair examination. For very general questions, it is almost impossible to help you direct your study efforts. What we can do is to point out some of the more common of these general abilities needed in public service positions and describe some typical questions.

1) General information

Broad, general information has been found useful for predicting job success in some kinds of work. This is tested in a variety of ways, from vocabulary lists to questions about current events. Basic background in some field of work, such as sociology or economics, may be sampled in a group of questions. Often these are principles which have become familiar to most persons through exposure rather than through formal training. It is difficult to advise you how to study for these questions; being alert to the world around you is our best suggestion.

2) Verbal ability

An example of an ability needed in many positions is verbal or language ability. Verbal ability is, in brief, the ability to use and understand words. Vocabulary and grammar tests are typical measures of this ability. Reading comprehension or paragraph interpretation questions are common in many kinds of civil service tests. You are given a paragraph of written material and asked to find its central meaning.

3) Numerical ability

Number skills can be tested by the familiar arithmetic problem, by checking paired lists of numbers to see which are alike and which are different, or by interpreting charts and graphs. In the latter test, a graph may be printed in the test booklet which you are asked to use as the basis for answering questions.

4) Observation

A popular test for law-enforcement positions is the observation test. A picture is shown to you for several minutes, then taken away. Questions about the picture test your ability to observe both details and larger elements.

5) Following directions

In many positions in the public service, the employee must be able to carry out written instructions dependably and accurately. You may be given a chart with several columns, each column listing a variety of information. The questions require you to carry out directions involving the information given in the chart.

6) Skills and aptitudes

Performance tests effectively measure some manual skills and aptitudes. When the skill is one in which you are trained, such as typing or shorthand, you can practice. These tests are often very much like those given in business school or high school courses. For many of the other skills and aptitudes, however, no short-time preparation can be made. Skills and abilities natural to you or that you have developed throughout your lifetime are being tested.

Many of the general questions just described provide all the data needed to answer the questions and ask you to use your reasoning ability to find the answers. Your best preparation for these tests, as well as for tests of facts and ideas, is to be at your physical and mental best. You, no doubt, have your own methods of getting into an exam-taking mood and keeping "in shape." The next section lists some ideas on this subject.

IV. KINDS OF QUESTIONS

Only rarely is the "essay" question, which you answer in narrative form, used in civil service tests. Civil service tests are usually of the short-answer type. Full instructions for answering these questions will be given to you at the examination. But in case this is your first experience with short-answer questions and separate answer sheets, here is what you need to know:

1) Multiple-choice Questions

Most popular of the short-answer questions is the "multiple choice" or "best answer" question. It can be used, for example, to test for factual knowledge, ability to solve problems or judgment in meeting situations found at work.

A multiple-choice question is normally one of three types—
- It can begin with an incomplete statement followed by several possible endings. You are to find the one ending which *best* completes the statement, although some of the others may not be entirely wrong.
- It can also be a complete statement in the form of a question which is answered by choosing one of the statements listed.

- It can be in the form of a problem – again you select the best answer.

Here is an example of a multiple-choice question with a discussion which should give you some clues as to the method for choosing the right answer:

When an employee has a complaint about his assignment, the action which will *best* help him overcome his difficulty is to
    A. discuss his difficulty with his coworkers
    B. take the problem to the head of the organization
    C. take the problem to the person who gave him the assignment
    D. say nothing to anyone about his complaint

In answering this question, you should study each of the choices to find which is best. Consider choice "A" – Certainly an employee may discuss his complaint with fellow employees, but no change or improvement can result, and the complaint remains unresolved. Choice "B" is a poor choice since the head of the organization probably does not know what assignment you have been given, and taking your problem to him is known as "going over the head" of the supervisor. The supervisor, or person who made the assignment, is the person who can clarify it or correct any injustice. Choice "C" is, therefore, correct. To say nothing, as in choice "D," is unwise. Supervisors have and interest in knowing the problems employees are facing, and the employee is seeking a solution to his problem.

2) True/False Questions

The "true/false" or "right/wrong" form of question is sometimes used. Here a complete statement is given. Your job is to decide whether the statement is right or wrong.

SAMPLE: A roaming cell-phone call to a nearby city costs less than a non-roaming call to a distant city.

This statement is wrong, or false, since roaming calls are more expensive.

This is not a complete list of all possible question forms, although most of the others are variations of these common types. You will always get complete directions for answering questions. Be sure you understand *how* to mark your answers – ask questions until you do.

V. RECORDING YOUR ANSWERS

Computer terminals are used more and more today for many different kinds of exams.
For an examination with very few applicants, you may be told to record your answers in the test booklet itself. Separate answer sheets are much more common. If this separate answer sheet is to be scored by machine – and this is often the case – it is highly important that you mark your answers correctly in order to get credit.

An electronic scoring machine is often used in civil service offices because of the speed with which papers can be scored. Machine-scored answer sheets must be marked with a pencil, which will be given to you. This pencil has a high graphite content which responds to the electronic scoring machine. As a matter of fact, stray dots may register as answers, so do not let your pencil rest on the answer sheet while you are pondering the correct answer. Also, if your pencil lead breaks or is otherwise defective, ask for another.

Since the answer sheet will be dropped in a slot in the scoring machine, be careful not to bend the corners or get the paper crumpled.

The answer sheet normally has five vertical columns of numbers, with 30 numbers to a column. These numbers correspond to the question numbers in your test booklet. After each number, going across the page are four or five pairs of dotted lines. These short dotted lines have small letters or numbers above them. The first two pairs may also have a "T" or "F" above the letters. This indicates that the first two pairs only are to be used if the questions are of the true-false type. If the questions are multiple choice, disregard the "T" and "F" and pay attention only to the small letters or numbers.

Answer your questions in the manner of the sample that follows:

32. The largest city in the United States is
    A. Washington, D.C.
    B. New York City
    C. Chicago
    D. Detroit
    E. San Francisco

1) Choose the answer you think is best. (New York City is the largest, so "B" is correct.)
2) Find the row of dotted lines numbered the same as the question you are answering. (Find row number 32)
3) Find the pair of dotted lines corresponding to the answer. (Find the pair of lines under the mark "B.")
4) Make a solid black mark between the dotted lines.

VI. BEFORE THE TEST

Common sense will help you find procedures to follow to get ready for an examination. Too many of us, however, overlook these sensible measures. Indeed, nervousness and fatigue have been found to be the most serious reasons why applicants fail to do their best on civil service tests. Here is a list of reminders:

- Begin your preparation early – Don't wait until the last minute to go scurrying around for books and materials or to find out what the position is all about.
- Prepare continuously – An hour a night for a week is better than an all-night cram session. This has been definitely established. What is more, a night a week for a month will return better dividends than crowding your study into a shorter period of time.
- Locate the place of the exam – You have been sent a notice telling you when and where to report for the examination. If the location is in a different town or otherwise unfamiliar to you, it would be well to inquire the best route and learn something about the building.
- Relax the night before the test – Allow your mind to rest. Do not study at all that night. Plan some mild recreation or diversion; then go to bed early and get a good night's sleep.
- Get up early enough to make a leisurely trip to the place for the test – This way unforeseen events, traffic snarls, unfamiliar buildings, etc. will not upset you.
- Dress comfortably – A written test is not a fashion show. You will be known by number and not by name, so wear something comfortable.

- Leave excess paraphernalia at home – Shopping bags and odd bundles will get in your way. You need bring only the items mentioned in the official notice you received; usually everything you need is provided. Do not bring reference books to the exam. They will only confuse those last minutes and be taken away from you when in the test room.
- Arrive somewhat ahead of time – If because of transportation schedules you must get there very early, bring a newspaper or magazine to take your mind off yourself while waiting.
- Locate the examination room – When you have found the proper room, you will be directed to the seat or part of the room where you will sit. Sometimes you are given a sheet of instructions to read while you are waiting. Do not fill out any forms until you are told to do so; just read them and be prepared.
- Relax and prepare to listen to the instructions
- If you have any physical problem that may keep you from doing your best, be sure to tell the test administrator. If you are sick or in poor health, you really cannot do your best on the exam. You can come back and take the test some other time.

VII. AT THE TEST

The day of the test is here and you have the test booklet in your hand. The temptation to get going is very strong. Caution! There is more to success than knowing the right answers. You must know how to identify your papers and understand variations in the type of short-answer question used in this particular examination. Follow these suggestions for maximum results from your efforts:

1) Cooperate with the monitor

The test administrator has a duty to create a situation in which you can be as much at ease as possible. He will give instructions, tell you when to begin, check to see that you are marking your answer sheet correctly, and so on. He is not there to guard you, although he will see that your competitors do not take unfair advantage. He wants to help you do your best.

2) Listen to all instructions

Don't jump the gun! Wait until you understand all directions. In most civil service tests you get more time than you need to answer the questions. So don't be in a hurry. Read each word of instructions until you clearly understand the meaning. Study the examples, listen to all announcements and follow directions. Ask questions if you do not understand what to do.

3) Identify your papers

Civil service exams are usually identified by number only. You will be assigned a number; you must not put your name on your test papers. Be sure to copy your number correctly. Since more than one exam may be given, copy your exact examination title.

4) Plan your time

Unless you are told that a test is a "speed" or "rate of work" test, speed itself is usually not important. Time enough to answer all the questions will be provided, but this does not mean that you have all day. An overall time limit has been set. Divide the total time (in minutes) by the number of questions to determine the approximate time you have for each question.

5) Do not linger over difficult questions

If you come across a difficult question, mark it with a paper clip (useful to have along) and come back to it when you have been through the booklet. One caution if you do this – be sure to skip a number on your answer sheet as well. Check often to be sure that you have not lost your place and that you are marking in the row numbered the same as the question you are answering.

6) Read the questions

Be sure you know what the question asks! Many capable people are unsuccessful because they failed to *read* the questions correctly.

7) Answer all questions

Unless you have been instructed that a penalty will be deducted for incorrect answers, it is better to guess than to omit a question.

8) Speed tests

It is often better NOT to guess on speed tests. It has been found that on timed tests people are tempted to spend the last few seconds before time is called in marking answers at random – without even reading them – in the hope of picking up a few extra points. To discourage this practice, the instructions may warn you that your score will be "corrected" for guessing. That is, a penalty will be applied. The incorrect answers will be deducted from the correct ones, or some other penalty formula will be used.

9) Review your answers

If you finish before time is called, go back to the questions you guessed or omitted to give them further thought. Review other answers if you have time.

10) Return your test materials

If you are ready to leave before others have finished or time is called, take ALL your materials to the monitor and leave quietly. Never take any test material with you. The monitor can discover whose papers are not complete, and taking a test booklet may be grounds for disqualification.

VIII. EXAMINATION TECHNIQUES

1) Read the general instructions carefully. These are usually printed on the first page of the exam booklet. As a rule, these instructions refer to the timing of the examination; the fact that you should not start work until the signal and must stop work at a signal, etc. If there are any *special* instructions, such as a choice of questions to be answered, make sure that you note this instruction carefully.

2) When you are ready to start work on the examination, that is as soon as the signal has been given, read the instructions to each question booklet, underline any key words or phrases, such as *least, best, outline, describe* and the like. In this way you will tend to answer as requested rather than discover on reviewing your paper that you *listed without describing*, that you selected the *worst* choice rather than the *best* choice, etc.

3) If the examination is of the objective or multiple-choice type – that is, each question will also give a series of possible answers: A, B, C or D, and you are called upon to select the best answer and write the letter next to that answer on your answer paper – it is advisable to start answering each question in turn. There may be anywhere from 50 to 100 such questions in the three or four hours allotted and you can see how much time would be taken if you read through all the questions before beginning to answer any. Furthermore, if you come across a question or group of questions which you know would be difficult to answer, it would undoubtedly affect your handling of all the other questions.

4) If the examination is of the essay type and contains but a few questions, it is a moot point as to whether you should read all the questions before starting to answer any one. Of course, if you are given a choice – say five out of seven and the like – then it is essential to read all the questions so you can eliminate the two that are most difficult. If, however, you are asked to answer all the questions, there may be danger in trying to answer the easiest one first because you may find that you will spend too much time on it. The best technique is to answer the first question, then proceed to the second, etc.

5) Time your answers. Before the exam begins, write down the time it started, then add the time allowed for the examination and write down the time it must be completed, then divide the time available somewhat as follows:
    - If 3-1/2 hours are allowed, that would be 210 minutes. If you have 80 objective-type questions, that would be an average of 2-1/2 minutes per question. Allow yourself no more than 2 minutes per question, or a total of 160 minutes, which will permit about 50 minutes to review.
    - If for the time allotment of 210 minutes there are 7 essay questions to answer, that would average about 30 minutes a question. Give yourself only 25 minutes per question so that you have about 35 minutes to review.

6) The most important instruction is to *read each question* and make sure you know what is wanted. The second most important instruction is to *time yourself properly* so that you answer every question. The third most important instruction is to *answer every question*. Guess if you have to but include something for each question. Remember that you will receive no credit for a blank and will probably receive some credit if you write something in answer to an essay question. If you guess a letter – say "B" for a multiple-choice question – you may have guessed right. If you leave a blank as an answer to a multiple-choice question, the examiners may respect your feelings but it will not add a point to your score. Some exams may penalize you for wrong answers, so in such cases *only*, you may not want to guess unless you have some basis for your answer.

7) Suggestions
    a. Objective-type questions
        1. Examine the question booklet for proper sequence of pages and questions
        2. Read all instructions carefully
        3. Skip any question which seems too difficult; return to it after all other questions have been answered
        4. Apportion your time properly; do not spend too much time on any single question or group of questions

5. Note and underline key words – *all, most, fewest, least, best, worst, same, opposite,* etc.
6. Pay particular attention to negatives
7. Note unusual option, e.g., unduly long, short, complex, different or similar in content to the body of the question
8. Observe the use of "hedging" words – *probably, may, most likely,* etc.
9. Make sure that your answer is put next to the same number as the question
10. Do not second-guess unless you have good reason to believe the second answer is definitely more correct
11. Cross out original answer if you decide another answer is more accurate; do not erase until you are ready to hand your paper in
12. Answer all questions; guess unless instructed otherwise
13. Leave time for review

   b. Essay questions
1. Read each question carefully
2. Determine exactly what is wanted. Underline key words or phrases.
3. Decide on outline or paragraph answer
4. Include many different points and elements unless asked to develop any one or two points or elements
5. Show impartiality by giving pros and cons unless directed to select one side only
6. Make and write down any assumptions you find necessary to answer the questions
7. Watch your English, grammar, punctuation and choice of words
8. Time your answers; don't crowd material

8) Answering the essay question

Most essay questions can be answered by framing the specific response around several key words or ideas. Here are a few such key words or ideas:

M's: manpower, materials, methods, money, management
P's: purpose, program, policy, plan, procedure, practice, problems, pitfalls, personnel, public relations

   a. Six basic steps in handling problems:
1. Preliminary plan and background development
2. Collect information, data and facts
3. Analyze and interpret information, data and facts
4. Analyze and develop solutions as well as make recommendations
5. Prepare report and sell recommendations
6. Install recommendations and follow up effectiveness

   b. Pitfalls to avoid
1. *Taking things for granted* – A statement of the situation does not necessarily imply that each of the elements is necessarily true; for example, a complaint may be invalid and biased so that all that can be taken for granted is that a complaint has been registered

2. *Considering only one side of a situation* – Wherever possible, indicate several alternatives and then point out the reasons you selected the best one
3. *Failing to indicate follow up* – Whenever your answer indicates action on your part, make certain that you will take proper follow-up action to see how successful your recommendations, procedures or actions turn out to be
4. *Taking too long in answering any single question* – Remember to time your answers properly

IX. AFTER THE TEST

Scoring procedures differ in detail among civil service jurisdictions although the general principles are the same. Whether the papers are hand-scored or graded by machine we have described, they are nearly always graded by number. That is, the person who marks the paper knows only the number – never the name – of the applicant. Not until all the papers have been graded will they be matched with names. If other tests, such as training and experience or oral interview ratings have been given, scores will be combined. Different parts of the examination usually have different weights. For example, the written test might count 60 percent of the final grade, and a rating of training and experience 40 percent. In many jurisdictions, veterans will have a certain number of points added to their grades.

After the final grade has been determined, the names are placed in grade order and an eligible list is established. There are various methods for resolving ties between those who get the same final grade – probably the most common is to place first the name of the person whose application was received first. Job offers are made from the eligible list in the order the names appear on it. You will be notified of your grade and your rank as soon as all these computations have been made. This will be done as rapidly as possible.

People who are found to meet the requirements in the announcement are called "eligibles." Their names are put on a list of eligible candidates. An eligible's chances of getting a job depend on how high he stands on this list and how fast agencies are filling jobs from the list.

When a job is to be filled from a list of eligibles, the agency asks for the names of people on the list of eligibles for that job. When the civil service commission receives this request, it sends to the agency the names of the three people highest on this list. Or, if the job to be filled has specialized requirements, the office sends the agency the names of the top three persons who meet these requirements from the general list.

The appointing officer makes a choice from among the three people whose names were sent to him. If the selected person accepts the appointment, the names of the others are put back on the list to be considered for future openings.

That is the rule in hiring from all kinds of eligible lists, whether they are for typist, carpenter, chemist, or something else. For every vacancy, the appointing officer has his choice of any one of the top three eligibles on the list. This explains why the person whose name is on top of the list sometimes does not get an appointment when some of the persons lower on the list do. If the appointing officer chooses the second or third eligible, the No. 1 eligible does not get a job at once, but stays on the list until he is appointed or the list is terminated.

X. HOW TO PASS THE INTERVIEW TEST

The examination for which you applied requires an oral interview test. You have already taken the written test and you are now being called for the interview test – the final part of the formal examination.

You may think that it is not possible to prepare for an interview test and that there are no procedures to follow during an interview. Our purpose is to point out some things you can do in advance that will help you and some good rules to follow and pitfalls to avoid while you are being interviewed.

What is an interview supposed to test?

The written examination is designed to test the technical knowledge and competence of the candidate; the oral is designed to evaluate intangible qualities, not readily measured otherwise, and to establish a list showing the relative fitness of each candidate – as measured against his competitors – for the position sought. Scoring is not on the basis of "right" and "wrong," but on a sliding scale of values ranging from "not passable" to "outstanding." As a matter of fact, it is possible to achieve a relatively low score without a single "incorrect" answer because of evident weakness in the qualities being measured.

Occasionally, an examination may consist entirely of an oral test – either an individual or a group oral. In such cases, information is sought concerning the technical knowledges and abilities of the candidate, since there has been no written examination for this purpose. More commonly, however, an oral test is used to supplement a written examination.

Who conducts interviews?

The composition of oral boards varies among different jurisdictions. In nearly all, a representative of the personnel department serves as chairman. One of the members of the board may be a representative of the department in which the candidate would work. In some cases, "outside experts" are used, and, frequently, a businessman or some other representative of the general public is asked to serve. Labor and management or other special groups may be represented. The aim is to secure the services of experts in the appropriate field.

However the board is composed, it is a good idea (and not at all improper or unethical) to ascertain in advance of the interview who the members are and what groups they represent. When you are introduced to them, you will have some idea of their backgrounds and interests, and at least you will not stutter and stammer over their names.

What should be done before the interview?

While knowledge about the board members is useful and takes some of the surprise element out of the interview, there is other preparation which is more substantive. It *is* possible to prepare for an oral interview – in several ways:

1) Keep a copy of your application and review it carefully before the interview

This may be the only document before the oral board, and the starting point of the interview. Know what education and experience you have listed there, and the sequence and dates of all of it. Sometimes the board will ask you to review the highlights of your experience for them; you should not have to hem and haw doing it.

2) Study the class specification and the examination announcement

Usually, the oral board has one or both of these to guide them. The qualities, characteristics or knowledges required by the position sought are stated in these documents. They offer valuable clues as to the nature of the oral interview. For example, if the job involves supervisory responsibilities, the announcement will usually indicate that knowledge of modern supervisory methods and the qualifications of the candidate as a supervisor will be tested. If so, you can expect such questions, frequently in the form of a hypothetical situation which you are expected to solve. NEVER go into an oral without knowledge of the duties and responsibilities of the job you seek.

3) Think through each qualification required

Try to visualize the kind of questions you would ask if you were a board member. How well could you answer them? Try especially to appraise your own knowledge and background in each area, *measured against the job sought*, and identify any areas in which you are weak. Be critical and realistic – do not flatter yourself.

4) Do some general reading in areas in which you feel you may be weak

For example, if the job involves supervision and your past experience has NOT, some general reading in supervisory methods and practices, particularly in the field of human relations, might be useful. Do NOT study agency procedures or detailed manuals. The oral board will be testing your understanding and capacity, not your memory.

5) Get a good night's sleep and watch your general health and mental attitude

You will want a clear head at the interview. Take care of a cold or any other minor ailment, and of course, no hangovers.

What should be done on the day of the interview?

Now comes the day of the interview itself. Give yourself plenty of time to get there. Plan to arrive somewhat ahead of the scheduled time, particularly if your appointment is in the fore part of the day. If a previous candidate fails to appear, the board might be ready for you a bit early. By early afternoon an oral board is almost invariably behind schedule if there are many candidates, and you may have to wait. Take along a book or magazine to read, or your application to review, but leave any extraneous material in the waiting room when you go in for your interview. In any event, relax and compose yourself.

The matter of dress is important. The board is forming impressions about you – from your experience, your manners, your attitude, and your appearance. Give your personal appearance careful attention. Dress your best, but not your flashiest. Choose conservative, appropriate clothing, and be sure it is immaculate. This is a business interview, and your appearance should indicate that you regard it as such. Besides, being well groomed and properly dressed will help boost your confidence.

Sooner or later, someone will call your name and escort you into the interview room. *This is it.* From here on you are on your own. It is too late for any more preparation. But remember, you asked for this opportunity to prove your fitness, and you are here because your request was granted.

What happens when you go in?

The usual sequence of events will be as follows: The clerk (who is often the board stenographer) will introduce you to the chairman of the oral board, who will introduce you to the other members of the board. Acknowledge the introductions before you sit down. Do not be surprised if you find a microphone facing you or a stenotypist sitting by. Oral interviews are usually recorded in the event of an appeal or other review.

Usually the chairman of the board will open the interview by reviewing the highlights of your education and work experience from your application – primarily for the benefit of the other members of the board, as well as to get the material into the record. Do not interrupt or comment unless there is an error or significant misinterpretation; if that is the case, do not hesitate. But do not quibble about insignificant matters. Also, he will usually ask you some question about your education, experience or your present job – partly to get you to start talking and to establish the interviewing "rapport." He may start the actual questioning, or turn it over to one of the other members. Frequently, each member undertakes the questioning on a particular area, one in which he is perhaps most competent, so you can expect each member to participate in the examination. Because time is limited, you may also expect some rather abrupt switches in the direction the questioning takes, so do not be upset by it. Normally, a board member will not pursue a single line of questioning unless he discovers a particular strength or weakness.

After each member has participated, the chairman will usually ask whether any member has any further questions, then will ask you if you have anything you wish to add. Unless you are expecting this question, it may floor you. Worse, it may start you off on an extended, extemporaneous speech. The board is not usually seeking more information. The question is principally to offer you a last opportunity to present further qualifications or to indicate that you have nothing to add. So, if you feel that a significant qualification or characteristic has been overlooked, it is proper to point it out in a sentence or so. Do not compliment the board on the thoroughness of their examination – they have been sketchy, and you know it. If you wish, merely say, "No thank you, I have nothing further to add." This is a point where you can "talk yourself out" of a good impression or fail to present an important bit of information. Remember, *you close the interview yourself.*

The chairman will then say, "That is all, Mr. _____, thank you." Do not be startled; the interview is over, and quicker than you think. Thank him, gather your belongings and take your leave. Save your sigh of relief for the other side of the door.

How to put your best foot forward

Throughout this entire process, you may feel that the board individually and collectively is trying to pierce your defenses, seek out your hidden weaknesses and embarrass and confuse you. Actually, this is not true. They are obliged to make an appraisal of your qualifications for the job you are seeking, and they want to see you in your best light. Remember, they must interview all candidates and a non-cooperative candidate may become a failure in spite of their best efforts to bring out his qualifications. Here are 15 suggestions that will help you:

1) Be natural – Keep your attitude confident, not cocky

If you are not confident that you can do the job, do not expect the board to be. Do not apologize for your weaknesses, try to bring out your strong points. The board is interested in a positive, not negative, presentation. Cockiness will antagonize any board member and make him wonder if you are covering up a weakness by a false show of strength.

2) Get comfortable, but don't lounge or sprawl

Sit erectly but not stiffly. A careless posture may lead the board to conclude that you are careless in other things, or at least that you are not impressed by the importance of the occasion. Either conclusion is natural, even if incorrect. Do not fuss with your clothing, a pencil or an ashtray. Your hands may occasionally be useful to emphasize a point; do not let them become a point of distraction.

3) Do not wisecrack or make small talk

This is a serious situation, and your attitude should show that you consider it as such. Further, the time of the board is limited – they do not want to waste it, and neither should you.

4) Do not exaggerate your experience or abilities

In the first place, from information in the application or other interviews and sources, the board may know more about you than you think. Secondly, you probably will not get away with it. An experienced board is rather adept at spotting such a situation, so do not take the chance.

5) If you know a board member, do not make a point of it, yet do not hide it

Certainly you are not fooling him, and probably not the other members of the board. Do not try to take advantage of your acquaintanceship – it will probably do you little good.

6) Do not dominate the interview

Let the board do that. They will give you the clues – do not assume that you have to do all the talking. Realize that the board has a number of questions to ask you, and do not try to take up all the interview time by showing off your extensive knowledge of the answer to the first one.

7) Be attentive

You only have 20 minutes or so, and you should keep your attention at its sharpest throughout. When a member is addressing a problem or question to you, give him your undivided attention. Address your reply principally to him, but do not exclude the other board members.

8) Do not interrupt

A board member may be stating a problem for you to analyze. He will ask you a question when the time comes. Let him state the problem, and wait for the question.

9) Make sure you understand the question

Do not try to answer until you are sure what the question is. If it is not clear, restate it in your own words or ask the board member to clarify it for you. However, do not haggle about minor elements.

10) Reply promptly but not hastily

A common entry on oral board rating sheets is "candidate responded readily," or "candidate hesitated in replies." Respond as promptly and quickly as you can, but do not jump to a hasty, ill-considered answer.

11) Do not be peremptory in your answers

A brief answer is proper – but do not fire your answer back. That is a losing game from your point of view. The board member can probably ask questions much faster than you can answer them.

12) Do not try to create the answer you think the board member wants

He is interested in what kind of mind you have and how it works – not in playing games. Furthermore, he can usually spot this practice and will actually grade you down on it.

13) Do not switch sides in your reply merely to agree with a board member

Frequently, a member will take a contrary position merely to draw you out and to see if you are willing and able to defend your point of view. Do not start a debate, yet do not surrender a good position. If a position is worth taking, it is worth defending.

14) Do not be afraid to admit an error in judgment if you are shown to be wrong

The board knows that you are forced to reply without any opportunity for careful consideration. Your answer may be demonstrably wrong. If so, admit it and get on with the interview.

15) Do not dwell at length on your present job

The opening question may relate to your present assignment. Answer the question but do not go into an extended discussion. You are being examined for a *new* job, not your present one. As a matter of fact, try to phrase ALL your answers in terms of the job for which you are being examined.

Basis of Rating

Probably you will forget most of these "do's" and "don'ts" when you walk into the oral interview room. Even remembering them all will not ensure you a passing grade. Perhaps you did not have the qualifications in the first place. But remembering them will help you to put your best foot forward, without treading on the toes of the board members.

Rumor and popular opinion to the contrary notwithstanding, an oral board wants you to make the best appearance possible. They know you are under pressure – but they also want to see how you respond to it as a guide to what your reaction would be under the pressures of the job you seek. They will be influenced by the degree of poise you display, the personal traits you show and the manner in which you respond.

ABOUT THIS BOOK

This book contains tests divided into Examination Sections. Go through each test, answering every question in the margin. We have also attached a sample answer sheet at the back of the book that can be removed and used. At the end of each test look at the answer key and check your answers. On the ones you got wrong, look at the right answer choice and learn. Do not fill in the answers first. Do not memorize the questions and answers, but understand the answer and principles involved. On your test, the questions will likely be different from the samples. Questions are changed and new ones added. If you understand these past questions you should have success with any changes that arise. Tests may consist of several types of questions. We have additional books on each subject should more study be advisable or necessary for you. Finally, the more you study, the better prepared you will be. This book is intended to be the last thing you study before you walk into the examination room. Prior study of relevant texts is also recommended. NLC publishes some of these in our Fundamental Series. Knowledge and good sense are important factors in passing your exam. Good luck also helps. So now study this Passbook, absorb the material contained within and take that knowledge into the examination. Then do your best to pass that exam.

EXAMINATION SECTION

EXAMINATION SECTION
TEST 1

DIRECTIONS: Each question or incomplete statement is followed by several suggested answers or completions. Select the one that BEST answers the question or completes the statement. *PRINT THE LETTER OF THE CORRECT ANSWER IN THE SPACE AT THE RIGHT.*

1. In programming, declaring a variable name involves what else other than naming?
   A. Type   B. Length   C. Size   D. Style

2. Name of a student is an example of
   A. operation
   B. method
   C. attribute
   D. none of the above

3. Basic strength of a computer is
   A. speed   B. memory   C. accuracy   D. reliability

4. *Only girls can become members of the committee. Many of the members of the committee are officers. Some of the officers have been invited for dinner.* Based on the above statements, which is the CORRECT conclusion?
   A. All members of the committee have been invited for the dinner.
   B. Some officers are not girls.
   C. All girls are the members of the committee.
   D. None of the above

5. Of the following statements, which of them cannot both be true and both be false?
   I.   All babies cry
   II. Some babies cry
   III. No babies cry
   IV. Some babies do not cry

   The CORRECT answer is:
   A. I and II   B. I and III   C. III and IV   D. I and IV

6. 3, 7, 15, 31, 63, ? What number should come next?
   A. 83   B. 127   C. 122   D. 76

7. If 30% of a number is 12.6, find the number?
   A. 45   B. 42   C. 54   D. 60

8. 10, 25, 45, 54, 60, 75, 80. The odd one out is
   A. 10   B. 45   C. 54   D. 60

9. Complement of an input is produced by which logical function?
   A. AND   B. OR   C. NOT   D. XOR

10. *If marks are greater than 70 and less than 85, then the grade is B.*
    This statement is an example of which programming control structure?
    A. Decision
    B. Loop
    C. Sequence
    D. None of the above

11. In programming, which operator is called the assignment operator?
    A. +
    B. =
    C. _
    D. %

12. In programming, which operator is called the modulus operator?
    A. +
    B. =
    C. %
    D. /

13. What is the correct order of running a computer program?
    A. Linking, loading, execution, translation
    B. Loading, translation, execution, linking
    C. Execution, translation, linking, loading
    D. Translation, loading, linking, execution

14. In the case of structure of programming, which of the following terms means "if none of the other statements are true"?
    A. Else
    B. Default
    C. While
    D. If

15. True statements:
    i. All benches are chairs.
    ii. Some chairs are desks.
    iii. All desks are pillars.
    Conclusions:
    I. Some pillars are benches.
    II. Some pillars are chairs.
    III. Some desks are benches.
    IV. No pillar is a bench.

    The CORRECT answer is:
    A. None of the above
    B. Either I or IV, and III
    C. Either I or IV
    D. Either I or IV, and II
    E. All of the above

16. True statements:
    i. Some snakes are reptiles.
    ii. All reptiles are poisonous.
    iii. Some poisonous reptiles are not snakes.
    Conclusions:
    I. Some poisonous reptiles are snakes.
    II. All snakes are poisonous.
    III. All reptiles are snakes.
    IV. No poisonous reptile is a snake.

    The CORRECT answer is:
    A. None of the above
    B. Either I or IV, and III
    C. Either I or IV, and II
    D. All of the above

17. Anna runs faster than Peter.
    Jane runs faster than Anna.
    Peter runs faster than Jane.
    If the first two statements are true, the third statement would be
      A. true   B. false   C. unknown   D. both

18. The sum of the digits of a two-digit number is 10. If the new number formed by reversing the digits is greater than the original number by 36, then what will be the original number?
      A. 37   B. 39   C. 57   D. 28

19. If an inverter is added to the output of an AND gate, what logic function is produced?
      A. AND   B. NAND   C. XOR   D. OR

20. Decimal 7 is represented by which gray code?
      A. 0111   B. 1011   C. 0100   D. 0101

21. According to propositional logic, if p = "A car costs less than $20,000", q = "David will buy a car."
    p → ~q refers to which of the following?
      A. If David will buy a car, the car costs less than $20,000.
      B. David will not buy a car if the car costs less than $20,000.
      C. David will buy a car if the car costs less than $20,000.
      D. None of the above

22. Which Boolean algebra rule is wrong?
      A. 0 + A = A   B. 0 + A = 1   C. A + A = A
      D. x • 1 = 1   E. All of the above

23. The 2's complement of 001011 is
      A. 110101   B. 010101   C. 110100   D. 010100

24. 7, 10, 8, 11, 9, 12. What number should come next?
      A. 12   B. 13   C. 8   D. 10

25. 2, 1, (1/2), (1/4). What number should come next?
      A. (1/16)   B. (1/8)   C. (2/8)   D. 1

KEY (CORRECT ANSWERS)

1.	A	11.	B
2.	C	12.	C
3.	B	13.	D
4.	D	14.	B
5.	B	15.	C
6.	B	16.	C
7.	B	17.	B
8.	C	18.	A
9.	C	19.	B
10.	A	20.	C

21. B
22. B
23. A
24. D
25. B

TEST 2

DIRECTIONS: Each question or incomplete statement is followed by several suggested answers or completions. Select the one that BEST answers the question or completes the statement. *PRINT THE LETTER OF THE CORRECT ANSWER IN THE SPACE AT THE RIGHT.*

1. 8, 27, 64, 100, 125, 216, 343. The odd one out is
    A. 343   B. 8   C. 27   D. 100

2. In programming, what is the operator precedence?
    A. Arithmetic, comparison, logical
    B. Comparison, arithmetic, logical
    C. Arithmetic, logical, comparison
    D. Logical, arithmetic, comparison

3. Which of the following is NOT a type of programming error?
    A. Logical   B. Syntax   C. Superficial   D. Runtime

4. Statements:
    i. No man is good.   ii. Jack is a man.
    Conclusions:
    I. Jack is not good   II. All men are not Jack.

    The CORRECT answer is:
    A. I
    B. II
    C. Either I or II
    D. Neither I nor II
    E. Both I and II

5. Statements:
    i. All students are boys.   ii. No boy is dull.
    Conclusions:
    I. There are no girls in the class.   II. No student is dull.

    The CORRECT answer is:
    A. I
    B. II
    C. Either I or II
    D. Neither I nor II
    E. Both I and II

6. What is the sum of two consecutive even numbers, the difference of whose squares is 84?
    A. 32   B. 36   C. 40   D. 42

7. Choose the odd one out:

   (1) (2) (3) (4)

   A. 1 B. 2 C. 3 D. 4

8. In the Netherlands, almost 200 cyclists die each year on the road.
   Head injury is the main cause of death among cyclists.
   Which of the following statements is true based on the above information?
   A. In the Netherlands, if wearing a helmet was widespread among cyclists, the number of deaths in cyclists could be reduced.
   B. Too many cyclists die each year on the road in the Netherlands.
   C. Most deaths in the Netherlands occur due to cycling.
   D. None of the above

9. According to propositional logic, what is the order of precedence of operators?
   A. ^, v, ↔, →
   B. ~, ^, v, →, ↔
   C. ~, v, ^, ↔, →
   D. →, ~, ^, v, ↔

10. The binary equivalent of the number 50 is
    A. 01101 B. 11010 C. 11100 D. 110010

11. Number 200 can be represented by how many bits?
    A. 1 B. 5 C. 8 D. 10

12. Which of the following is NOT true?
    A. 0 × 0 = 0 B. 1 × 0 = 0 C. 0 × 1 = 1 D. 1 × 1 = 1

13. Get two numbers
    If first number is bigger than second then
    Print first number
    Else
    Print second number
    The above pseudo-code is an example of which control structure?
    A. Loop
    B. Sequence
    C. Decision
    D. None of the above

14. A group of variables is called
    A. data structure
    B. control structure
    C. data object
    D. linked list

15. The first character of the string variable St is represented by
    A. St[1]
    B. St[0]
    C. St
    D. none of the above

16. Statements:
    i. No girl is poor   B. All girls are rich
    Conclusions:
    I. No poor girl is rich   II. No rich girl is poor

    The CORRECT answer is:
    A. I   B. II
    C. Either I or II   D. Neither I nor II
    E. Both I and II

17. Statements:
    i. All fishes are orange in color   ii. Some fishes are heavy
    Conclusions:
    I. All heavy fishes are orange in color
    II. All light fishes are not orange in color

    The CORRECT answer is:
    A. I   B. II
    C. Either I or II   D. Neither I nor II
    E. Both I and II

18. 3, 7, 6, 5, 9, 3, 12, 1, 15. What number should come next?
    A. 18   B. 13   C. 1   D. -1

19. 5184, 1728, 576, 192. What number should come next?
    A. 64   B. 32   C. 120   D. 44

20. $(p \Leftrightarrow r) \Rightarrow (q \Leftrightarrow r)$ is equivalent to
    A. $[(\sim p \vee r) \wedge (p \vee \sim r)] \vee \sim [(\sim q \vee r) \wedge (q \vee \sim r)]$
    B. $\sim[(\sim p \vee r) \wedge (p \vee \sim r)] \vee [(\sim q \vee r) \wedge (q \vee \sim r)]$
    C. $[(\sim p \vee r) \wedge (p \vee \sim r)] \wedge [(\sim q \vee r) \wedge (q \vee \sim r)]$
    D. $[(\sim p \vee r) \wedge (p \vee \sim r)] \vee [(\sim q \vee r) \wedge (q \vee \sim r)]$

21. Which of the following propositions is a tautology?
    A. $(p \vee q) \to q$ B. $p \vee (q \to p)$ C. $p \vee (p \to q)$ D. b & c

22. According to propositional logic, if p = "Mary gets an A in computer science", q = "Mary got 90% marks in computer science."
    p ↔ q refers to which of the following?
    A. Mary gets an A in computer science if and only if her percentage in computer science is 90%.
    B. Mary might get an A in computer science if her percentage in computer science is 90%
    C. Mary get an A in computer science if her percentage in computer science is 90%.
    D. None of the above

23. What does the following flowchart depict?   23.____

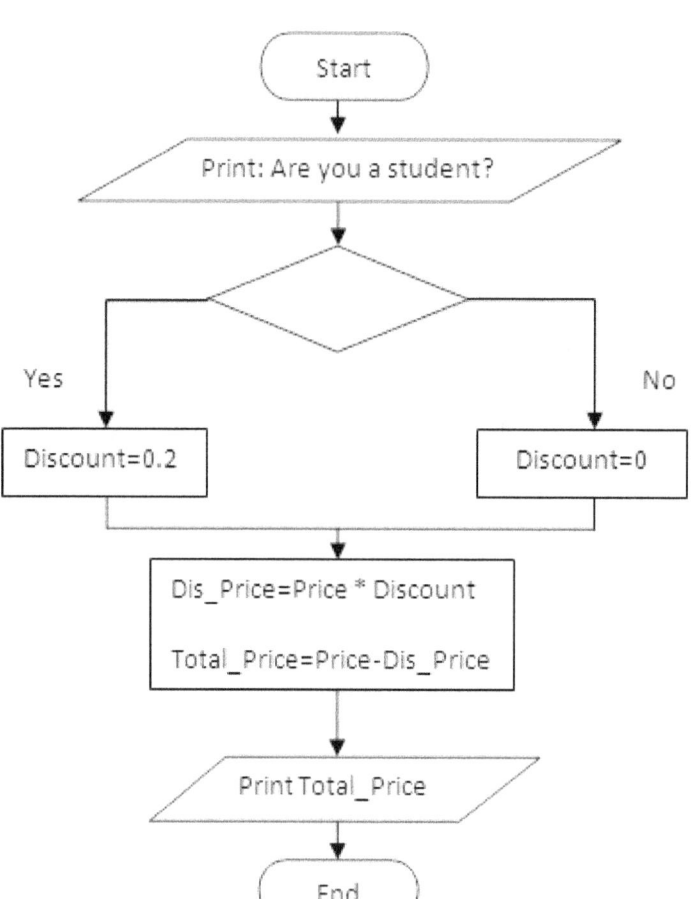

   A. All users get a discount.
   B. If user is a student, only then does he get a discount.
   C. If user is a student, he does not get a discount, while other users get a discount.
   D. None of the above

24. 13, 35, 57, 79, 911. What number should come next?   24.____
   A. 1113   B. 1114   C. 1100   D. 1111

25. Choose the missing shape.

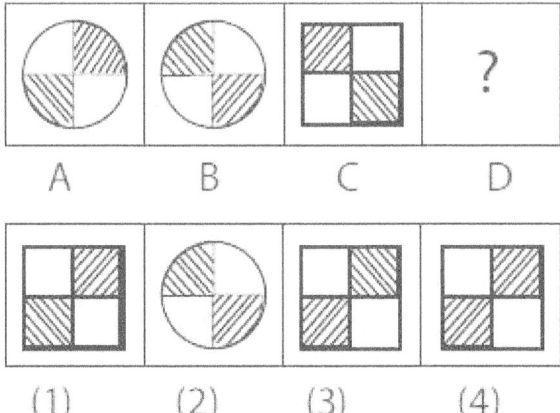

A. 1   B. 2   C. 3   D. 4

KEY (CORRECT ANSWERS)

1. D   11. C
2. A   12. C
3. C   13. C
4. A   14. A
5. E   15. B

6. D   16. E
7. A   17. A
8. A   18. D
9. B   19. A
10. D   20. B

21. D
22. A
23. B
24. C
25. C

TEST 3

DIRECTIONS: Each question or incomplete statement is followed by several suggested answers or completions. Select the one that BEST answers the question or completes the statement. *PRINT THE LETTER OF THE CORRECT ANSWER IN THE SPACE AT THE RIGHT.*

1. The following flowchart represents which control structure? 1.____

   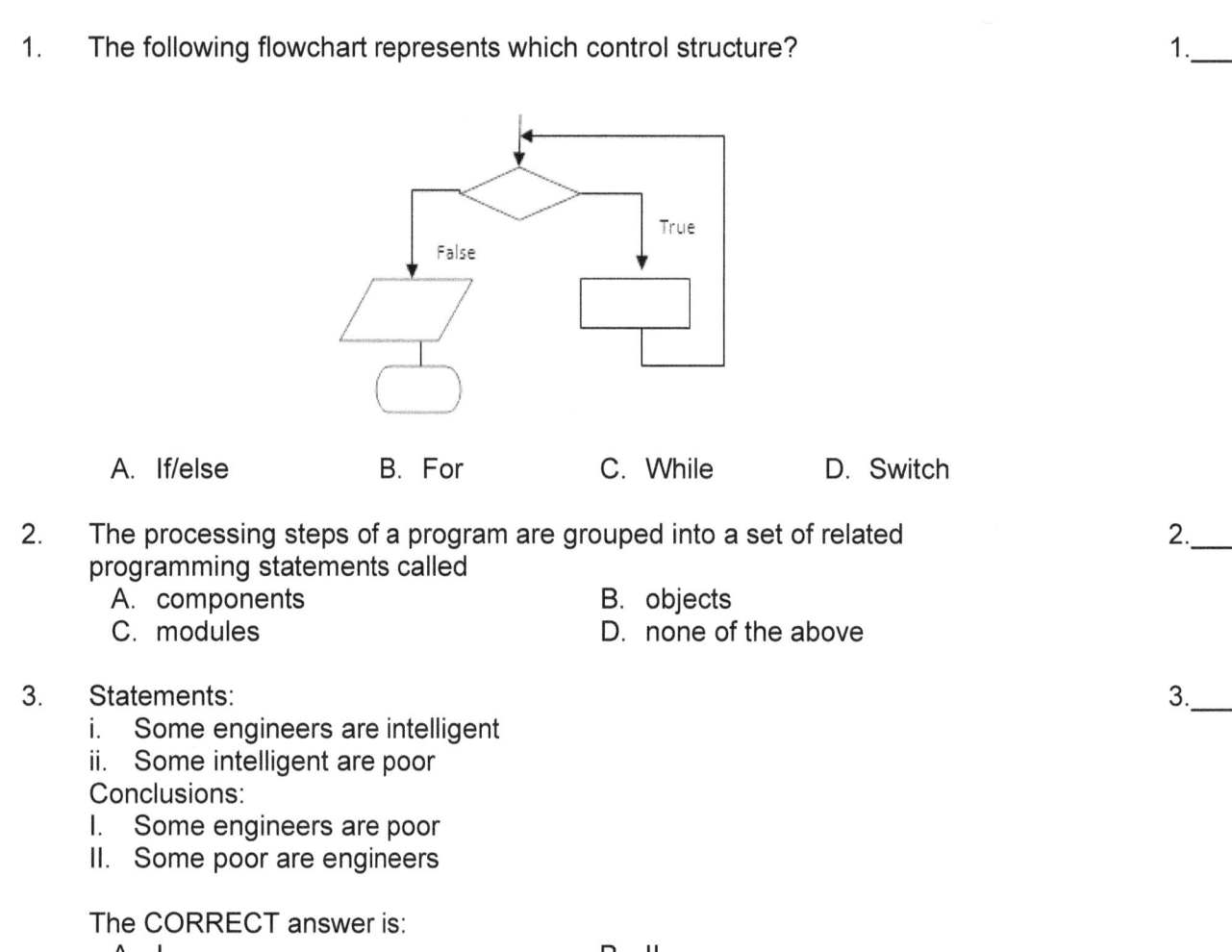

   A. If/else   B. For   C. While   D. Switch

2. The processing steps of a program are grouped into a set of related programming statements called 2.____
   - A. components
   - B. objects
   - C. modules
   - D. none of the above

3. Statements: 3.____
   i. Some engineers are intelligent
   ii. Some intelligent are poor
   Conclusions:
   I. Some engineers are poor
   II. Some poor are engineers

   The CORRECT answer is:
   - A. I
   - B. II
   - C. Either I or II
   - D. Neither I nor II
   - E. Both I and II

4. Statements: 4.____
   i. No man is a fool   ii. John is a man
   Conclusions:
   I. John is not a fool   II. All men are not John

   The CORRECT answer is:
   - A. I
   - B. II
   - C. Either I or II
   - D. Neither I nor II
   - E. Both I and II

5. John weighs less than Fred.
John weighs more than Boomer.
Of the three dogs, Boomer weighs the least.

If the first two statements are true, the third statement is
A. true B. false C. uncertain D. both

6. A file contains 10 sheets and none of these sheets is blue. Which of the following statements can be deduced?
   A. None of the 10 sheets contained in the file are blue.
   B. The file contains a blue sheet.
   C. The file contains at least one yellow sheet.
   D. None of the above

7. Choose the odd one out:

   (1) (2) (3) (4)

   A. 1 B. 2 C. 3 D. 4

8. Which of the following structures requires the statements to be repeated until a condition is met?
   A. Sequence   B. If....Else
   C. For   D. None of the above

9. While n is greater than 0
   Increment count
   end
   The above pseudo-code represents which programming structure?
   A. Sequence   B. Loop
   C. Structure   D. None of the above

10. Which of the following converts a source code into machine code and turns it into an exe file?
    A. Linker   B. Compiler
    C. Interpreter   D. None of the above

11. Which of the following is used to hide data and its functionality?
    A. Structure   B. Loop
    C. Object   D. Selection statement

12. Statements:
    i. All apples are golden in color
    ii. No golden colored things are cheap
    Conclusions:
    I. All apples are cheap
    II. Golden colored apples are not cheap

    The CORRECT answer is:
    A. I
    B. II
    C. Either I or II
    D. Neither I nor II
    E. Both I and II

13. Statements:
    i. All cups are glasses
    ii. All glasses are bowls
    iii. No bowl is a plate
    Conclusions:
    I. No cup is a plate
    II. No glass is a plate
    III. Some plates are bowls
    IV. Some cups are not glasses

    The CORRECT answer is:
    A. None of the above
    B. Either I or IV, and III
    C. Either I or IV
    D. Either I or IV, and II
    E. All of the above

14. 331, 482, 551, 263, 383, 362, 284. The odd one out is
    A. 331 B. 383 C. 284 D. 551

15. 3, 5, 7, 12, 17, 19. The odd one out is
    A. 7 B. 17 C. 12 D. 19

16. Ratio of 12 minutes to 1 hour is:
    A. 2:3 B. 1:5 C. 1:6 D. 1:8

17. 10 cats caught 10 rats in 10 seconds. How many cats are required to catch 100 rats in 100 seconds?
    A. 100 B. 50 C. 200 D. 10

18. Four engineers and six technicians can complete a project in 8 days, while three engineers and seven technicians can complete it in 10 days. In how many days will ten technicians complete it?
    A. 40 B. 36 C. 50 D. 45

19. According to propositional logic, if p = "Jane is smart", "q = "Jane is honest", then p v (~p ^ q) refers to which of the following?
    A. Either Jane is smart or honest.
    B. Jane is smart and honest.
    C. Either Jane is smart, or she is not smart but honest.
    D. None of the above

20. In binary number system, the number 102 is equal to
    A. 1100110   B. 1001100   C. 1110110   D. 1100101

21. In base 8, number 362 is represented as
    A. 550   B. 552   C. 545   D. 566

22. 396, 462, 572, 427, 671, 264. The odd one out is
    A. 427   B. 572   C. 671   D. 264

23. A is two years older than B who is twice as old as C. If the total of the ages of A, B and C is 27, then how old is B?
    A. 10   B. 11   C. 12   D. 13

24. What is 50% of 40% of Rs. 3,450?
    A. 580   B. 670   C. 690   D. 570

25. What is the minimum number of colors required to fill the spaces in the following diagram without the adjacent sides having the same color?

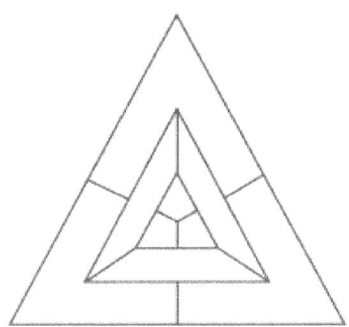

    A. 3
    C. 6
    B. 4
    D. Not possible to determine

KEY (CORRECT ANSWERS)

1.	A	11.	A
2.	C	12.	B
3.	E	13.	A
4.	A	14.	D
5.	A	15.	C
6.	A	16.	B
7.	D	17.	D
8.	C	18.	A
9.	B	19.	C
10.	B	20.	A

21. B
22. A
23. A
24. C
25. A

TEST 4

DIRECTIONS: Each question or incomplete statement is followed by several suggested answers or completions. Select the one that BEST answers the question or completes the statement. *PRINT THE LETTER OF THE CORRECT ANSWER IN THE SPACE AT THE RIGHT.*

1. Computer signals that include both measuring and counting are called 1.____
   A. analog   B. digital
   C. hybrid   D. none of the above

2. The result of ANDing 5 and 4 is 2.____
   A. 30   B. 9
   C. 20   D. none of the above

3. If one wants to trace an organization's purchase orders from creation to final disposition, he should use which of the following? 3.____
   A. Data flow diagram   B. Internal control flow chart
   C. System flow chart   D. Program flow chart

4. Statements: 4.____
   i. Some tables are sofas   ii. All furniture are tables
   Conclusions:
   I. Some furniture are sofas   II. Some sofas are furniture

   The two statements given should be assumed to be true. Select the conclusion.
   A. I   B. II
   C. Either I or II   D. Neither I nor II
   E. Both I and II

5. Statements: 5.____
   i. Many actors are singers.   ii. All singers are dancers.
   Conclusions:
   I. Some actors are dancers.   II. No singer is an actor.

   The CORRECT answer is:
   A. I   B. II
   C. Either I or II   D. Neither I nor II
   E. Both I and II

6. Anna will not pass both the verbal reasoning test and quantitative reasoning test. This statement refers to which of the following? 6.____
   A. Anna will not pass the verbal reasoning test.
   B. Anna will neither pass quantitative reasoning test nor verbal reasoning test.
   C. Anna will pass either the verbal reasoning test or the numerical reasoning test.
   D. If Anna passes the verbal reasoning test, she will not pass the numerical reasoning test.

7. Which symbol is used at the beginning of the flowchart?

   A. ◯   B. ⬭   C. ◇   D. ▭

8. A list of instructions in a proper order to solve a problem is called
   A. sequence
   B. algorithm
   C. flowchart
   D. none of the above

9. Statements:
   i. Some pearls are stones
   ii. Some stones are diamonds
   iii. No diamond is a gem
   Conclusions:
   I. Some gems are pearls
   II. Some gems are diamonds
   III. No gem is a diamond
   IV. No gem is a pearl

   The CORRECT answer is:
   A. None of the above
   B. Either I or IV, and III
   C. Either I or IV
   D. Either I or IV, and II
   E. All of the above

10. 53, 53, 40, 40, 27, 27. What number should come next?
    A. 14   B. 12   C. 13   D. 10

11. 1, 3, 1, 9, 1, 81, 1. What number should come next?
    A. 4   B. 1   C. 343   D. 6561

12. A father is 30 years older than his son. He will be three times as old as his son after 5 years. What is the father's present age?
    A. 30   B. 35   C. 40   D. 45

13. Ahmed is older than Ali
    Maria is older than Ahmed.
    Ali is older than Maria.
    If the first two statements are true, the third statement is
    A. true   B. false   C. unknown   D. both

14. All flowers are fruit.
    Some flowers are leaves.
    All leaves are fruit.
    If the first two statements are true, the third statement is
    A. true   B. false   C. unknown   D. both

15. The Spring Mall has more stores than the Four Seasons Mall.
    The Four Corners Mall has fewer stores than the Four Seasons Mall.
    The Spring Mall has more stores than the Four Corners Mall.
    If the first two statements are true, the third statement is
    A. true   B. false   C. unknown   D. both

16. Choose the odd one out:

    A. 1 B. 2 C. 3 D. 4

17. Fact 1: All cats like to jump.
    Fact 2: Some cats like to run.
    Fact 3: Some cats look like dogs.
    If the first three statements are true, which of the following statements must also be true?
    I. All cats who like to jump look like dogs.
    II. Cats who like to run also like to jump.
    III. Cats who like to jump do not look like dogs.

    The CORRECT answer is:
    A. I only
    B. II only
    C. II and III only
    D. None of the above

18. Fact 1: All chickens are birds.
    Fact 2: Some chickens are hens.
    Fact 3: Female birds lay eggs.
    If the first three statements are true, which of the following statements must also be true?
    I. All birds lay eggs.
    II. Some hens are birds.
    III. Some chickens are not hens.

    The CORRECT answer is:
    A. I only
    B. II only
    C. II and III only
    D. None of the above

19. Fact 1: Jake has four watches.
    Fact 2: Two of the watches are black.
    Fact 3: One of the watches is a Rolex.
    If the first three statements are true, which of the following statements must also be true?
    I. Jake has a Rolex.
    II. Jake has three watches.
    III. Jake's favorite color is black.

    The CORRECT answer is:
    A. I only
    B. II only
    C. II and III only
    D. None of the above

20. Which symbol of a flowchart is used to test a condition?   20.____

    A. ◯   B. ▱   C. ◇   D. ⬭

21. Which symbol of a flowchart is used for input and output?   21.____

    A. ◯   B. ▱   C. ◇   D. ▭

22. Which of the following is NOT one of the categories of flowcharting symbols?   22.____
    A. Input/output symbols   B. Processing symbols
    C. Storage symbols   D. Flow symbols

23. Choose the missing shape.   23.____

    A. 1   B. 2   C. 3   D. 4

24. Choose the missing shape.   24.____

    A. 1   B. 2   C. 3   D. 4

25. How many minimum numbers of colors will be required to fill a cube without adjacent sides having the same color? 25.____
    A. 3   B. 4   C. 6   D. 8

KEY (CORRECT ANSWERS)

1. C
2. C
3. B
4. E
5. A

6. B
7. B
8. B
9. B
10. A

11. D
12. C
13. B
14. C
15. A

16. A
17. B
18. B
19. A
20. C

21. B
22. C
23. B
24. A
25. A

EXAMINATION SECTION
TEST 1

DIRECTIONS: Each question or incomplete statement is followed by several suggested answers or completions. Select the one that BEST answers the question or completes the statement. *PRINT THE LETTER OF THE CORRECT ANSWER IN THE SPACE AT THE RIGHT.*

1. The purpose of the _____ module is to show the overall flow of data through a program.   1._____

    A. file maintenance
    B. read
    C. control
    D. init

2. An index file consists of the _____ fields.   2._____

    A. key and record number
    B. name and masterfile
    C. date and counter
    D. record number and data address

3. Which of the following is/are used to specify detailed computer operations to implement functions?   3._____

    A. Pseudocode
    B. Structure charts
    C. Data flow charts
    D. Modules

4. The purpose of programming an array into an information system is to allow the user to   4._____

    A. practice random file access
    B. sequentially update files
    C. store several values for the same variable in the internal memory of the computer
    D. access any number of variables without having to script

5. What is the MOST commonly used logic structure in systems programming?   5._____

    A. Decision
    B. Sequential
    C. Case
    D. Loop

6. The _____ module enters data into a program.   6._____

    A. init   B. read   C. control   D. write

7. Control-break modules serve to _____ in systems programming.   7._____

    A. interrupt processing in case of a logic error
    B. transfer data from one processing path to another
    C. interrupt processing in case of a data error
    D. give subtotals for a group of similar records

8. The normal order in which modules are presented to the computer and activated are called   8._____

    A. repetitions
    B. selections
    C. sequences
    D. case constructs

9. The EASIEST to program is the

   A. bubble sort
   B. binary search
   C. sequential search
   D. merge of two lists

10. The instruction to increment a variable by one would be written

    A. COUNTER = COUNTER + 1
    B. SUM = COUNTER + 1
    C. COUNTER = SUM + 1
    D. SUM = SUM + VARIABLE

11. A programmer should create a(n) _____ file for storing completed file updates.

    A. transaction
    B. activity
    C. backup
    D. temporary

12. For the purpose of data validation, a new module will need to be processed from the _____ module.

    A. READ
    B. WRAPUP
    C. CALC
    D. WRITE

13. A _____ module is NOT a type of process data module.

    A. control
    B. print
    C. calculation
    D. read

14. In a written computer solution or program flowchart, a marker is used to indicate that there are no more records to be processed.
    This marker is

    A. EXIT
    B. HF
    C. EOF
    D. END

15. The PRIMARY reason negative logic is used in systems programming is to

    A. provide a way of thinking that is more convenient for people
    B. provide a means for checking data validity
    C. increase the number of variables
    D. decrease the number of tests

16. When creating a random-access information system, a programmer sometimes *chains* modules on top of each other. The purpose of this is to

    A. make the program more interactive
    B. place data in intermediate storage of input and output, to speed up processing
    C. enable the user to use larger programs, and leave more room for data in the internal memory
    D. process all the necessary tasks after files have been updated and processed

17. An information system is programmed to put a mailing list into both alphabetical and zip code order.
    What type of logic structure will be used to program the system?

    A. Decision
    B. Case
    C. Sequential
    D. Loop

18. Which of the following is BASIC code used to disassociate a data file from a program?

    A. END
    B. DATA
    C. CLOSE
    D. DIM

19. Which of the following is used to load an array?

    A. WRITE module B. Loop
    C. String   D. Primer read

20. Which of the following is NOT a type of decision logic used in the programming structure?

    A. True   B. False
    C. Conditional   D. Straight-through

21. _____ are tools primarily of the case logic structure.

    A. Decision tables B. Codes
    C. READ modules   D. Variables

22. What type of operator, within an expression or equation, uses numerical or string data as operands, and produces logical data as the resultant?

    A. Relational   B. Network
    C. Logical   D. Hierarchical

23. In a program flowchart, an assignment instruction would be written

    A. LET   B. VARIABLE=
    C. READ   D. WRITE AS

24. When a programmer wants the value in one array to point to an element in another array, he uses

    A. a null file   B. a primer read
    C. a nested loop   D. the pointer technique

25. The purpose of _____ is to eliminate rewriting of identical system processes.

    A. pseudocode   B. sequences
    C. repetitions   D. modules

KEY (CORRECT ANSWERS)

1. C
2. A
3. A
4. C
5. B

6. B
7. D
8. C
9. C
10. A

11. B
12. A
13. A
14. C
15. D

16. C
17. D
18. C
19. B
20. C

21. B
22. A
23. B
24. D
25. D

TEST 2

DIRECTIONS: Each question or incomplete statement is followed by several suggested answers or completions. Select the one that BEST answers the question or completes the statement. *PRINT THE LETTER OF THE CORRECT ANSWER IN THE SPACE AT THE RIGHT.*

1. What is the term for the summation of values within nonsignificant data fields, such as keys and identification number fields?   1.____

    A. Accumulation   B. Hash total
    C. Null files   D. Entry key total

2. The PRIMARY purpose of indicators is to   2.____

    A. maintain the processing of a loop structure
    B. change the processing path
    C. assist in nesting loops or decisions
    D. assist in detecting logic errors

3. Which of the following is NOT a means of converting positive logic to negative logic?   3.____

    A. Changing all <= to >
    B. Changing all < to >
    C. Changing all >= to <
    D. Interchanging all of the THEN set of instructions with the corresponding ELSE set of instructions

4. A programmer writes the instruction SUM = SUM + A(R) into a program flowchart, with R = the number of a specific element in an array, and A(R) = the Rth element of the array. The purpose of this instruction is to   4.____

    A. multiply the data items in an array by the number of elements
    B. incrementalize the elements in an array
    C. accumulate the data items in an array
    D. accumulate the elements in an array

5. The term for altering the normal sequential execution of program statements is   5.____

    A. branching   B. trailing   C. interrupting   D. indicating

6. By using the _____ logic structure, a programmer can enable a user to enter the value of a variable from the keyboard, or from a file, to select one of several options in a list.   6.____

    A. loop   B. sequential   C. case   D. decision

7. Which of the following is BASIC code used to define and reserve areas within memory to be used as program tables?   7.____

    A. RETURN   B. IF   C. REM   D. DIM

8. If a programmer overlays sections of a program on top of each other, she will also have to create a(n) _____ to access any of the modules when requested.   8.____

    A. control module   B. driver program
    C. string editor   D. nested loop

25

9. A HOLD instruction will be supplied for _____ modules.

   A. control-break   B. end
   C. wrapup   D. init

10. Data is initially recorded, prior to system input, on a form called the

    A. b-tree   B. primer buffer
    C. source document   D. init module

11. The _____ module processes instructions only once during a program, and only at the beginning.

    A. init   B. control   C. wrapup   D. read

12. A programmer should place all data needed to update a master file into a(n) _____ file.

    A. temporary   B. transaction
    C. read   D. backup

13. Which of the following instructions is used PRIMARILY in a loop logic structure?

    A. REPEAT/UNTIL   B. END/EXIT
    C. PROCESS   D. IF/THEN

14. Program processing ends at a point called the

    A. physical end   B. control-break
    C. logical end   D. hash point

15. A company maintains a sequential-accessible database. In the record data dictionary, each of the following items would be created as string data EXCEPT

    A. district number   B. sales amount
    C. sales date   D. salesperson name

16. In systems programming and design, developing the _____ would occur FIRST.

    A. IPO chart   B. algorithms
    C. structure chart   D. flowcharts

17. In a program flowchart, a temporary file is usually represented as

    A. HF   B. TEMP   C. F<   D. TF

18. The instruction to accumulate a variable A would be written

    A. COUNTER = A + 1   B. SUM = COUNTER + A
    C. COUNTER = SUM + A   D. SUM = SUM + A

19. In order to distinguish data items or data fields as separate entities, a programmer uses a symbol known as a(n)

    A. hash mark   B. null character
    C. delimiter   D. cursor

20. If a program uses the loop logic structure, the programmer must create a(n) _____ to   20.____
    enter data to process before the loop begins.
    A. primer read   B. clear all
    C. INIT module   D. PROCESS module

21. Each array location is known as a(n)   21.____
    A. stack   B. element
    C. string   D. linked list

22. Which of the following is BASIC code used to link a data file to a program?   22.____
    A. LINK   B. OPEN   C. LET   D. GOTO

23. IF/THEN/ELSE instructions are used in programs that use the _____ logic structure.   23.____
    A. case   B. loop   C. decision   D. array

24. A(n) _____ is used in program problem-solving to stand for a memory location at which   24.____
    a data value is retained.
    A. array   B. variable   C. cell   D. element

25. Which of the following is NOT a type of indicator used in systems programming?   25.____
    A. Trip value   B. Switch
    C. Nested loop   D. Flag

KEY (CORRECT ANSWERS)

1. B　　11. A
2. B　　12. B
3. B　　13. A
4. D　　14. C
5. A　　15. B

6. C　　16. C
7. D　　17. A
8. B　　18. D
9. A　　19. C
10. C　　20. A

21. B
22. B
23. C
24. B
25. C

EXAMINATION SECTION
TEST 1

DIRECTIONS: Each question or incomplete statement is followed by several suggested answers or completions. Select the one that BEST answers the question or completes the statement. *PRINT THE LETTER OF THE CORRECT ANSWER IN THE SPACE AT THE RIGHT.*

1. In defining a program, the analyst reviews the   1.____
    - A. data flow diagram
    - B. module definitions
    - C. system specifications
    - D. analysis walkthrough
    - E. All of the above

2. During program definition, the analyst determines the   2.____
    - A. programming language to be used
    - B. programmers that will code the programs
    - C. name of each program
    - D. purpose of each program
    - E. All of the above

3. In reviewing each circle in the data flow diagram, the analyst will find it yields a   3.____
    - A. data flow
    - B. program
    - C. need for a vendor
    - D. need for a computer operator
    - E. All of the above

4. Each circle in the data flow diagram is identified by a   4.____
    - A. square
    - B. letter
    - C. number
    - D. rectangle
    - E. file name

5. Circles in the data flow diagram will have data inflows and   5.____
    - A. program names
    - B. data compression
    - C. data concentration
    - D. data outflows
    - E. file names

6. Circles in a data flow diagram will have   6.____
    - A. data inflows
    - B. names
    - C. numbers
    - D. data outflows
    - E. All of the above

7. Programs are divided into   7.____
    - A. models
    - B. modules
    - C. sentences
    - D. pseudocode
    - E. divisions

8. A module has a(n)   8.____
    - A. single entry point
    - B. single exit point
    - C. single function
    - D. finite length
    - E. All of the above

9. Module length should be restricted to 24

    A. pages
    B. keystrokes
    C. lines
    D. words
    E. sentences

10. Modularizing is

    A. a part of the structured methodology
    B. a programming language sentence
    C. control structure
    D. repetition structure
    E. coupling method

11. Which of the following is NOT a control structure?

    A. Sequence
    B. Function
    C. Decision
    D. Repetition
    E. All are control structures

12. Which control structure permits testing of values and alternative conditions?

    A. Sequence
    B. Decomposition
    C. Decision
    D. Repetition
    E. Solution

13. Which control structure describes a linear series of actions?

    A. Sequence
    B. Decomposition
    C. Decision
    D. Repetition
    E. Solution

14. Which control structure represents a loop?

    A. Sequence
    B. Decomposition
    C. Decision
    D. Repetition
    E. Solution

15. Which control structure is also known as IF-THEN-ELSE?

    A. Decision
    B. Refinement
    C. Sequence
    D. Decomposition
    E. Repetition

16. Which control structure is also known as WHILE-DO?

    A. Decision
    B. Refinement
    C. Sequence
    D. Decomposition
    E. Repetition

17. Which control structure is also known as REPEAT-UNTIL?

    A. Decision
    B. Refinement
    C. Sequence
    D. Decomposition
    E. Repetition

18. Which control structure is also known as CASE?

    A. Decision
    B. Refinement
    C. Sequence
    D. Decomposition
    E. Repetition

19. The breaking down of a system or module into its elementary components is called

    A. decision
    B. refinement
    C. sequence
    D. lowering
    E. none of the above

20. A synonym for refinement is

   A. decision
   B. sequence
   C. levelling
   D. coupling
   E. recomposition

KEY (CORRECT ANSWERS)

1.	A	11.	B
2.	E	12.	C
3.	B	13.	A
4.	C	14.	D
5.	D	15.	A
6.	E	16.	E
7.	B	17.	E
8.	E	18.	A
9.	C	19.	B
10.	A	20.	C

TEST 2

DIRECTIONS: Each question or incomplete statement is followed by several suggested answers or completions. Select the one that BEST answers the question or completes the statement. *PRINT THE LETTER OF THE CORRECT ANSWER IN THE SPACE AT THE RIGHT.*

1. Which term stands for the inter-relationship among modules?

    A. Coupling
    B. Cascading
    C. Cohesion
    D. Levelling
    E. Refinement

2. What type of coupling do independent modules exhibit?

    A. Tight
    B. Loose
    C. Data
    D. Stamp
    E. Control

3. What type of coupling do dependent modules exhibit?

    A. Tight
    B. Loose
    C. Data
    D. Stamp
    E. Control

4. Which programming instruction violates the single entry/exit function concept of structured methodology?

    A. PERFORM
    B. READ
    C. GO TO
    D. WRITE
    E. STOP

5. Modules should read from

    A. left to bottom
    B. top down
    C. bottom up
    D. right to left
    E. None of the above

6. Which of the following is NOT a criteria in module design?

    A. Identification of system dependent functions
    B. Module length
    C. Single entry/exit/purpose
    D. Minimization of reference to data
    E. None of the above

7. Which of the following is NOT a criteria in module design?

    A. Constructing loosely coupled modules
    B. Avoiding content coupled modules
    C. Testing module cohesion
    D. Naming functions according to their purpose
    E. None of the above

8. Which language is the MOST widely used for business applications?

    A. FORTRAN
    B. BASIC
    C. COBOL
    D. Ada
    E. Pascal

9. Which language is now supported as *the* language of the Department of Defense?

    A. FORTRAN
    B. BASIC
    C. COBOL
    D. Ada
    E. Pascal

10. Which language is MOST often used on home or personal computers? 10.____

    A. FORTRAN   B. BASIC   C. COBOL
    D. Ada   E. Pascal

11. Which language is MOST often the one first-year computer science majors learn? 11.____

    A. FORTRAN   B. BASIC   C. COBOL
    D. Ada   E. Pascal

12. Which of the following is NOT a part of system specifications? 12.____

    A. System overview
    B. Data flow diagram
    C. Output or report designs
    D. Database or schema design
    E. None of the above

13. Which of the following is NOT a part of program specifications? 13.____

    A. Module descriptions   B. Program definitions
    C. Module pseudocode   D. Module names
    E. None of the above

14. The review of the second phase of the systems process is called the 14.____

    A. analysis walkthrough   B. system audit
    C. design walkthrough   D. development walkthrough
    E. design overview

15. A design review attempts to locate errors in 15.____

    A. screen formats
    B. costs forecast during analysis
    C. benefits predicted during analysis
    D. management decisions made during analysis
    E. All of the above

16. Outputs from the design review include . 16.____

    A. management discussions
    B. direction to progress to development
    C. direction to progress to analysis
    D. system overview
    E. All of the above

17. Who authorizes the development phase of the systems process? 17.____

    A. Users   B. Programmers   C. Analyst
    D. Management   E. All of the above

18. Modularizing a program makes it easier to 18.____

    A. compile   B. write Ada statements
    C. read   D. write assignment statements
    E. All of the above

19. Modularizing makes it easier to
    A. spot potential errors in the COBOL syntax
    B. spot errors in logic
    C. place responsibility for errors
    D. assign staff for testing
    E. All of the above

20. Which of the following is NOT an output from design?
    A. System specifications
    B. Module descriptions
    C. Program specifications
    D. Database design
    E. COBOL programs

KEY (CORRECT ANSWERS)

1.	A		11.	E
2.	B		12.	E
3.	A		13.	E
4.	C		14.	C
5.	B		15.	A
6.	E		16.	B
7.	E		17.	D
8.	C		18.	C
9.	D		19.	B
10.	B		20.	E

EXAMINATION SECTION
TEST 1

DIRECTIONS: Each question or incomplete statement is followed by several suggested answers or completions. Select the one that BEST answers the question or completes the statement. *PRINT THE LETTER OF THE CORRECT ANSWER IN THE SPACE AT THE RIGHT.*

1. Development begins after the analyst receives

    A. management's approval of the system analysis
    B. management's approval of the design review
    C. user's approval of the design review
    D. user's review of the system specifications
    E. management's review of the system specifications

2. Which of the following is development more like?

    A. Consultations with an architect
    B. Consultations with a builder
    C. Construction of a home
    D. Drawing of blueprints
    E. Moving into a new home

3. Which of the following is design more like?

    A. Consultations with an architect
    B. Consultations with a builder
    C. Construction of a home
    D. Drawing of blueprints
    E. Moving into a new home

4. Which of the following is NOT a part of development?

    A. Database design
    B. User training
    C. Conversion
    D. Testing
    E. All are a part of development

5. Which of the following is NOT a part of development?

    A. Programming
    B. User training
    C. Conversion
    D. Testing
    E. All are a part of development

6. Which of the following is the LAST task performed during development?

    A. User training   B. System audit
    C. Conversion   D. Operations training
    E. System documentation

7. Which of the following is the FIRST task performed during development?

    A. User training
    B. System audit
    C. Review and assignment of tasks
    D. Operations training
    E. System documentation

8. An implementation plan is a(n)

    A. outline of tasks to be performed
    B. outline of modules to be written
    C. list of programs to be written
    D. schedule of design tasks
    E. none of the above

9. Which tool is an analyst likely to use in scheduling development activities?

    A. Schema   B. Data dictionary
    C. HIPO chart   D. PERT chart
    E. VTOC

10. Which tool is an analyst likely to use in scheduling development activities?

    A. Gantt chart   B. Data dictionary
    C. HIPO chart   D. IPO chart
    E. VTOC

11. Standards are USUALLY established to

    A. promote consistency in programming style
    B. ease program maintenance
    C. make programs more readable
    D. ease training of new staff members
    E. All of the above

12. Programming or coding begins

    A. *after* programs are defined
    B. *after* modules are defined
    C. *after* testing begins
    D. *before* modules are defined
    E. *after* reviewing the system specifications

13. A stub is a

    A. completely written module
    B. pair of modules
    C. partially written module
    D. COBOL verb
    E. none of the above

14. Programmers create stubs to   14.____

    A. take the place of the DATA DIVISION of a COBOL program
    B. set aside modules for another programmer to write
    C. test completely written modules
    D. set aside a module for later coding
    E. all of the above

15. Programmers create stubs to   15.____

    A. permit early testing
    B. permit modules to be written in any order
    C. allow concentration on crucial modules first
    D. boost morale
    E. all of the above

16. An alternative to the top-down program construction is   16.____

    A. left-to-right   B. right-to-left   C. bottom-up
    D. inside-out   E. outside-in

17. A program walkthrough finds   17.____

    A. errors in analysis
    B. errors in database design
    C. proper language use
    D. improper language use
    E. all of the above

18. A program walkthrough finds   18.____

    A. errors in language use   B. faulty logic
    C. omissions   D. errors in file names
    E. all of the above

19. Faulty logic appears as   19.____

    A. a spelling error
    B. forgetting to call a specific procedure
    C. a program that does not function as intended
    D. a forgotten MOVE statement
    E. all of the above

20. Improper language use appears as   20.____

    A. a spelling error
    B. forgetting to call a specific procedure
    C. a program that does not function as intended
    D. a forgotten MOVE statement
    E. all of the above

KEY (CORRECT ANSWERS)

1. B
2. C
3. D
4. A
5. E

6. B
7. C
8. A
9. D
10. A

11. E
12. B
13. C
14. D
15. E

16. C
17. D
18. E
19. C
20. A

TEST 2

DIRECTIONS: Each question or incomplete statement is followed by several suggested answers or completions. Select the one that BEST answers the question or completes the statement. *PRINT THE LETTER OF THE CORRECT ANSWER IN THE SPACE AT THE RIGHT.*

1. An omission appears as 1.____

    A. a spelling error
    B. forgetting to call a specific procedure
    C. a program that does not function as intended
    D. a forgotten MOVE statement in building a print line
    E. All of the above

2. Program walkthroughs take place 2.____

    A. *after* testing
    B. *after* coding
    C. *before* database design
    D. *after* training
    E. at any time

3. Module testing checks 3.____

    A. the correctness of a module
    B. the placement of the module in the program
    C. module coupling
    D. the sequence of programs relative to each other
    E. the sequence of programs relative to modules

4. Modules integration checks 4.____

    A. the correctness of a module
    B. the placement of the module in the program
    C. module coupling
    D. the sequence of programs relative to each other
    E. the sequence of programs relative to modules

5. Program testing checks 5.____

    A. the correctness of a module
    B. the placement of the module in the program
    C. module coupling
    D. the sequence of programs relative to each other
    E. the sequence of programs relative to modules

6. Module testing is also known as 6.____

    A. cohesion tests   B. unit testing
    C. program integration   D. user testing
    E. module training

39

7. Data to test programs or modules can be

   A. extracted from the old system
   B. made up by the programmer
   C. generated by the user
   D. generated by the computer
   E. All of the above

8. When writing IF statements,

   A. ELSE's should be matched with other ELSE's
   B. ELSE's should be paired with GO TO's
   C. ELSE's should match IF's
   D. IF's should be matched with other IF's
   E. All of the above

9. A well-constructed IF statement should

   A. pair each IF with an ELSE
   B. use parenthesis to identify conditions
   C. avoid over 5 levels of IF's
   D. not be over 24 lines long
   E. All of the above

10. GO TO's should

    A. be minimized
    B. match EXIT's
    C. be placed liberally in the program
    D. lead to the middle of a module
    E. lead to the end of the program

11. Parallel conversion requires _____ system(s).

    A. immediately abandoning the current
    B. gradual replacement of the current
    C. simultaneous operation of two
    D. simultaneous operation of two manual
    E. None of the above

12. Direct conversion requires _____ system(s).

    A. immediately abandoning the current
    B. gradual replacement of the current
    C. simultaneous operation of two
    D. simultaneous operation of two manual
    E. None of the above

13. Phased conversion requires _____ system(s).

    A. immediately abandoning the current
    B. gradual replacement of the current
    C. simultaneous operation of two

D. simultaneous operation of two manual
E. None of the above

14. Cut, slash, or cold-turkey conversion requires _____ system(s).   14._____

    A. immediately abandoning the current
    B. gradual replacement of the current
    C. simultaneous operation of two
    D. simultaneous operation of two manual
    E. None of the above

15. Besides converting data to a new system, the analyst may also need to modify   15._____

    A. costs
    B. the type of tape drive on the computer
    C. facilities
    D. management decision-making processes
    E. All of the above

16. Besides converting data to a new system, the analyst may also need to modify   16._____

    A. procedure
    B. the type of tape drive on the computer
    C. the faculty
    D. management decision-making processes
    E. All of the above

17. Besides converting data to a new system, the analyst may also need to write special pur-   17._____
    pose

    A. data
    B. programs
    C. facilities
    D. management decision-making instructions
    E. All of the above

18. Modifying an old COBOL routine for a new system is an example of which type of conver-   18._____
    sion?

    A. Facilities   B. Program   C. Data
    D. Procedures   E. All of the above

19. Installing raised flooring in the computer center is an example of which type of conver-   19._____
    sion?

    A. Facilities   B. Program   C. Data
    D. Procedures   E. All of the above

20. Instituting new rules or regulations for a new system is an example of which type of con-   20._____
    version?

    A. Facilities   B. Program   C. Data
    D. Procedures   E. All of the above

KEY (CORRECT ANSWERS)

1. D
2. B
3. A
4. C
5. D

6. B
7. E
8. C
9. E
10. A

11. C
12. A
13. B
14. A
15. C

16. A
17. B
18. B
19. A
20. D

EXAMINATION SECTION
TEST 1

DIRECTIONS: Each question or incomplete statement is followed by several suggested answers or completions. Select the one that *BEST* answers the question or completes the statement. *PRINT THE LETTER OF THE CORRECT ANSWER IN THE SPACE AT THE RIGHT.*

1. Data Processing is the

    A. input and output of data
    B. transformation of data into information
    C. production of computer generated reports
    D. collection and dissemination of data
    E. none of the above

2. The CORRECT hierarchy of data is

    A. field, file, record, database
    B. character, field, record, file, database
    C. record, file, field, database
    D. bit, byte, record, database
    E. character, file, record, field, database

3. Which of the following is an update operation?

    A. Adding data
    B. Deleting data
    C. Changing data
    D. All of the above
    E. None of the above

4. The _____ are three MAIN components of a computer generated report.

    A. Control breaks, summaries and headings
    B. Detail lines, control breaks and graphs
    C. Headings, detail lines and summary lines
    D. Page breaks, headings and control breaks
    E. Columns, rows and totals

5. A computer generated report with control breaks must have

    A. the data organized in random order
    B. the data being produced from at least two files
    C. the data sorted on a control field
    D. page breaks on each control field
    E. at least two control breaks to be meaningful

6. The *primary* types of data processing environments in existence today are

    A. batch and real-time
    B. real-time and on-line
    C. transaction and batch
    D. batch and on-line
    E. on-line and real-time

7. The FIRST step in solving a problem with a computer is

   A. coding
   B. debugging
   C. problem analysis
   D. system analysis
   E. problem definition with tools such as flowcharts or data flow diagrams

8. In the hierarchy of arithmetic operations, the operation with the HIGHEST priority is

   A. addition
   B. multiplication
   C. exponentiation
   D. parenthesis
   E. division

9. If A = 10, B = 20 and C - 30, what would be the result of the following operation?
   A * B + C * A

   A. 2,300
   B. 500
   C. 400
   D. 3,000
   E. none of these

10. If A = 5, B = 10 and C = 15, what would be the result of the following operation?
    A + C / (C + A)

    A. 1   B. 5.75   C. C, 10.5   D. 20   E. 15

11. A(n) _____ is a formula developed to solve a problem.

    A. computer program
    B. algorithm
    C. flowchart
    D. problem definition
    E. all of the above

12. The two MAIN data types are

    A. numeric and non-numeric
    B. alphabetic and alphanumeric
    C. numeric and alphabetic
    D. arithmetic and logical
    E. alphabetic and special characters

Questions 13 - 19

DIRECTIONS: Use the following flowchart symbols to answer questions 13-19.

13. Which is used for commenting flowcharts? 13_____

14. Which is a process symbol? 14_____

15. Which is a decision box? 15_____

16. Which is a terminal? 16_____

17. Which is an input output symbol? 17_____

18. Which symbol would be BEST suited for the following expression? Is A > B? 18_____

19. Which symbol would be BEST suited for the following expression? Let tax = sale-price * .08? 19_____

20. An advantage of using a flowchart is that 20_____

    A. it is easy to update
    B. it is well suited for long problems
    C. its symbols are very easily memorized
    D. it graphically represents a problem
    E. all of the above are advantages

21. Flowcharting does NOT indicate 21_____

    A. flow lines   B. sequence
    C. line numbers   D. repetition or looping
    E. logical operations

22. A _____ keeps and maintains the content and description of variable names, file, and field names. 22_____

    A. database   B. data dictionary
    C. encyclopedia of data   D. data descriptor
    E. computer program

23. The _____ is the part of a program which may be repeated. 23_____

    A. loop   B. data structure
    C. repetition structure   D. logic structure
    E. subroutine structure

24. Employee gross-pay is calculated by multiplying hours by rate. A tax rate of 8% is deducted before arriving at net-pay. 24_____
    Which equation would describe the calculation of gross-pay?

    A. Gross-pay = hours * rate * tax-rate
    B. Gross-pay = hours * rate - tax-rate
    C. Gross-pay = (hours * rate) - .08
    D. Gross-pay = 8 - (hours * rate)
    E. None of these

25. If you deposit $1,000 in a savings account at 8% interest for one year, at the end of the year there will be $1,080.
Which equation would determine the amount in the bank? Amount = 1000*

    A. 8   B. .08   C. 108   D. 1.08   E. 8%

25___

KEY (CORRECT ANSWERS)

1. B
2. B
3. D
4. C
5. C

6. D
7. C
8. D
9. B
10. B

11. B
12. A
13. D
14. A
15. C

16. B
17. E
18. C
19. A
20. D

21. C
22. B
23. A
24. E
25. D

TEST 2

DIRECTIONS: Each question or incomplete statement is followed by several suggested answers or completions. Select the one that *BEST* answers the question or completes the statement. *PRINT THE LETTER OF THE CORRECT ANSWER IN THE SPACE AT THE RIGHT.*

1. The three *primary* program logic structures are   1____

    A. looping, branching and sequence
    B. sequence, selection and iteration
    C. arithmetic, logic and sequence
    D. looping, sequence and logic
    E. arithmetic, logic and branching

2. Two basic symbols used by hierarchy charts are   2____

    A. flow lines and circles
    B. process blocks (rectangles) End squares
    C. decision boxes and flow lines
    D. parallelograms and flow lines
    E. flow lines and process blocks (rectangles)

3. A _____ is a violation of the rules made by the programmer.   3____

    A. logic error   B. structure error
    C. syntax error   D. bug
    E. slip

4. _____ verifies transaction data at all input, processing, and output points.   4____

    A. Verification   B. An audit trail
    C. A transaction log   D. A transaction journal
    E. A ledger

5. _____ file organization arranges files in input sequence.   5____

    A. Random   B. Direct
    C. Sequential   D. Relative
    E. Indexed

6. _____ refers to the process of examining a program design and reviewing the logic of a program with test data.   6____

    A. Debugging   B. Desk checking
    C. Stepwise refinement   D. Verification
    E. Logic testing

7. This type of file organization allows a single record to be accessed without accessing the entire file. The location of the record to be accessed is relative to the position of the first record in the file. This paragraph refers to _____ access.   7____

    A. direct   B. random
    C. serial   D. relative
    E. indexed

8. A _____ is a variable which will keep track of the number of occurrences of a certain transaction.

   A. counter
   B. accumulator
   C. totaler
   D. tally
   E. register

9. The _____ report will list all or most of the information in a file.

   A. summary
   B. detail
   C. transaction
   D. exception
   E. monitor

10. Data is *originally* recorded in the _____ document.

    A. transaction
    B. object
    C. original
    D. source
    E. master

11. This verification technique confirms that data being input meets certain input criteria. The data being entered may be compared to a list of values.
    This paragraph refers to the

    A. range test
    B. matching values
    C. control totals
    D. required field
    E. class test

12. This verification technique confirms that data falls within certain limit of values.
    This statement refers to the

    A. range test
    B. matching values
    C. control totals
    D. required field
    E. class test

13. The binary (base 2) symbol equivalent to the decimal (base 10) number 31 is

    A. 31   B. 1111   C. 11111   D. 1011   E. none of these

14. The binary (base 2) symbol equivalent to the decimal (base 10) number 13 is

    A. 1011   B. 1010   C. 1101   D. 1100   E. none of these

15. The decimal (base 10) symbol equivalent to the binary (base 2) number 11101 is

    A. 13   B. 24   C. 19   D. 30   E. none of these

16. The hexadecimal (base 16) symbol equivalent to the decimal (base 10) number 2605 is

    A. A2D
    B. 3402
    C. 101000101101
    D. B6C
    E. none of the above

17. The hexadecimal symbol equivalent to the decimal (base 10) number 59 is

    A. 4A   B. A4   C. 3B   D. B3   E. none of these

18. The binary (base 2) symbol equivalent to the hexadecimal value 4D3CE is

A. 01000000111101010000 B. 00110101110010110001
C. 10001101110010001100 D. 01001101001111001110
E. none of the above

19. The hexadecimal (base 16) symbol equivalent to the binary (base 2) number 100010011010 is

    A. 82C   B. 74   C. AC1
    D. 89A   E. none of these

20. The octal (base 8) symbol equivalent to the binary (base 2) number 101111011001 is

    A. BD9   B. 42   C. 18
    D. 5731   E. none of these

21. Consider the following input data: John, O Reilly, Johnson, O'Reilly. If a computer were to arrange these names according to the standard collating sequence, the output would be

    A. Johnson, John, O Reilly, O'Reilly
    B. John, Johnson, O'Reilly, O Reilly
    C. O'Reilly, O Reilly, Johnson, John
    D. John, Johnson, O Reilly, O'Reilly
    E. both a or c

22. In reference to the diagram below, this flowchart sequence describes

    A. conditional flow   B. branching   C. repetitive flow
    D. logical flow   E. sequential flow

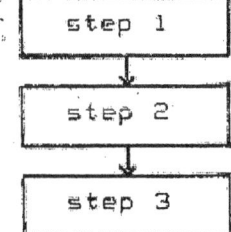

23. Which of the following comparisons would result in a true outcome?

    A. 5 = 10 or 6 = 5 and 8 = 2
    B. 10 = 12 and 6=6
    C. 7 = 4 or 9 = 9 and 4 = 4
    D. 5 = 5 and 3 = 2 or 7 = 7
    E. none of the above

24. Which of the following comparisons would result in a true outcome?

    A. 5 > 6 and 8 > 4
    B. 5 > 6 or 4 > 8
    C. 10 = 10 and 8 < 4 or 8 < 3
    D. 67 = 67 and 101 < 345 or 3 = 9
    E. none of the above

25. Which of the following comparisons would result in a true outcome?

    A. 5 = 6 or 7 < 3
    B. (10 < 12 or 14 = 15) and 9=9
    C. (17 > 10 or 5 < 6) and 5 > 7
    D. 88< = 88 and 99 < 98
    E. none of the above

25____

KEY (CORRECT ANSWERS)

1.	B	11.	B
2.	E	12.	A
3.	C	13.	C
4.	B	14.	C
5.	C	15.	E
6.	B	16.	A
7.	D	17.	C
8.	A	18.	D
9.	B	19.	D
10.	D	20.	D

21.	D
22.	E
23.	C
24.	D
25.	B

EXAMINATION SECTION
TEST 1

DIRECTIONS: Each question or incomplete statement is followed by several suggested answers or completions. Select the one that BEST answers the question or completes the statement. *PRINT THE LETTER OF THE CORRECT ANSWER IN THE SPACE AT THE RIGHT.*

1. All computer programs must contain four types of commands. Which of the following is NOT one of these types?   1._____

   A. Diagnostic B. Input
   C. Operations D. Output

2. In machine language, the symbol for a base register is   2._____

   A. X   B. Y   C. Z   D. A

3. Which of the following programming languages is used PRIMARILY for science applications?   3._____

   A. COBOL   B. FORTRAN   C. ADRS-II   D. Pascal

4. The purpose of an object program is to   4._____

   A. detect syntax errors in an assembly-language program
   B. pass assembly-language instructions to the link editor
   C. correct bit errors in a machine language
   D. define the ultimate outcome for a high-level programming language

5. The MOST basic type of programming language is   5._____

   A. FORTRAN   B. machine code
   C. assembly language   D. BASIC

6. Each of the following is an advantage associated with the use of machine language EXCEPT   6._____

   A. immediately executable instructions
   B. efficient use of computer storage
   C. manipulation of individual bits by instructions
   D. relative ease in design and writing

7. In a program flowchart, a priming read serves to   7._____

   A. clear spurious code from the processor
   B. initialize accumulators to zero
   C. check the placement of decision branches
   D. fetch an initial data item for processing

8. Which of the following functions is represented by the program flowchart symbol shown at the right?   8._____

   A. Preparation
   B. Processing
   C. Input/output
   D. Connector

51

9. Which of the following is NOT a component of machine language?

    A. Register number
    B. Operation code
    C. Operand
    D. Data address

10. What symbol is used on a printer layout form to represent numeric information?

    A. ∞
    B. A
    C. X
    D. #

11. Desk-checking is a process used to detect _____ errors in a computer program.

    A. run-time
    B. logic
    C. operational
    D. syntax

12. The purpose of assembly language is to

    A. provide the source code for a program
    B. write the binary code for each instruction
    C. translate high-level language instructions into machine code
    D. condense machine code instructions into simpler instructions

13. Each of the following is a disadvantage associated with the use of assembly languages EXCEPT

    A. machine-dependency
    B. not immediately executable
    C. programmers must memorize addresses of data values
    D. high correspondence between assembly-language instructions and machine-language instructions

14. The process of a program's executing the same instructions again and again is known as

    A. repeating
    B. looping
    C. jamming
    D. reversion

15. Run-time errors result in

    A. unpredictable program glitches
    B. an outright failure of the program to run
    C. consistent performance of undesired tasks
    D. the program running at the wrong speed

16. In an assembly language, the location of data values in primary memory is given by the

    A. operand field
    B. label field
    C. operation code
    D. data address

17. Which of the following programming languages is particularly suited for searching through large business files?

    A. FORTRAN
    B. BASIC
    C. COBOL
    D. Pascal

18. Which of the following is NOT a disadvantage associated with the use of HIPO charts?

    A. Extensive programmer training and experience required
    B. Concentration on what is to be accomplished, rather than how to accomplish it
    C. Use of top-down programming techniques
    D. Extra documentation requirements

19. Which of the following functions is represented by the program flowchart symbol shown at the right?

    A. Off-page connector
    B. Terminal
    C. Processing
    D. Annotation

19.____

20. The purpose of a register number is to

    A. signify which register to use when computational procedures are required
    B. tell the control unit what data-processing operation is to be performed
    C. construct a base register for each instruction
    D. locate elements in the computer's primary memory

20.____

21. Syntax errors occur when

    A. the source code is translated incorrectly
    B. the program performs a task, but it is not the task that was desired
    C. a compiler is not used
    D. a language command is spelled incorrectly

21.____

22. In machine language, the symbol for an index register is

    A. X   B. Y   C. Z   D. A

22.____

23. When using BASIC to get a directory of files, a user should type

    A. CD   B. dir   C. FILES   D. LIST

23.____

24. A _____ is a set of print statements or screen-display statements whose output enables a programmer to follow a computer's processing path during execution.

    A. trace routine   B. desk-check
    C. control total   D. control break

24.____

25. In order to translate a program written in a high-level language into machine code, a(n) _____ is used.

    A. assembler   B. calculator
    C. compiler   D. translator

25.____

KEY (CORRECT ANSWERS)

1.	A	11.	B
2.	B	12.	D
3.	B	13.	C
4.	A	14.	B
5.	B	15.	A
6.	D	16.	A
7.	D	17.	C
8.	A	18.	C
9.	C	19.	B
10.	C	20.	A

21. D
22. A
23. C
24. A
25. C

TEST 2

DIRECTIONS: Each question or incomplete statement is followed by several suggested answers or completions. Select the one that BEST answers the question or completes the statement. *PRINT THE LETTER OF THE CORRECT ANSWER IN THE SPACE AT THE RIGHT.*

1. Which of the following programming languages has a very precise structure that is particularly good for training serious programmers? 1.____

   A. Encore B. Pascal C. APL D. FORTRAN

2. The purpose of symbols in an assembly language is to 2.____

   A. tell the control unit what processing task to perform
   B. help document the program
   C. mark correspondence between a value in a formula and memory locations containing that value
   D. represent memory locations

3. Which of the following languages is *interpreted* rather than compiled? 3.____

   A. BASIC B. COBOL C. FORTRAN D. Pascal

4. Each of the following is an advantage associated with the use of assembly languages EXCEPT 4.____

   A. easier to use than machine languages
   B. ability to combine several data-processing steps into one
   C. useful for detecting program errors
   D. encouragement of modular programming

5. _____ is represented by the program flowchart symbol shown at the right. 5.____

   A. Decision
   B. Preparation
   C. Predefined process
   D. Input/output

6. The purpose of an operation code is to 6.____

   A. signify which register to use when computational procedures are required
   B. tell the control unit what data-processing operation is to be performed
   C. construct a base register for each instruction
   D. locate elements in the computer's primary memory

7. What symbol is used on a printer layout form to represent alphabetic information? 7.____

   A. *f* B. A C. X D. Δ

8. Which of the following is NOT a component instruction of an assembly language? 8.____

   A. Operand   B. Operation code
   C. Register number D. Name

55

9. Each of the following is an advantage associated with BASIC EXCEPT

   A. good error diagnostics
   B. real-time coding
   C. easy to use
   D. self-structured

10. A(n) _____ is used to translate a program into machine code every time the program is run.

    A. translator
    B. interpreter
    C. compiler
    D. assembler

11. Which of the following is NOT a disadvantage associated with the use of machine languages?

    A. Poor programmer productivity
    B. Machine-dependency
    C. Required control of each register in arithmeticlogic unit
    D. Storage locations cannot be addressed directly

12. Each of the following is one of the major divisions of all COBOL programs EXCEPT

    A. coding
    B. identification
    C. data
    D. environment

13. Which of the following programming languages is capable of treating alphabetic text as a set of logic statements?

    A. LISP
    B. ADA
    C. FORTRAN
    D. APL

14. Which of the following is NOT an advantage associated with the use of the RPG language?

    A. Inexpensive programming
    B. Problem-oriented
    C. Widely compatible with different machines
    D. Easy to code

15. Logic errors occur when

    A. the source code is translated back into machine language
    B. the program performs a task, but it is not the task that was desired
    C. an assembler is not used
    D. a language command is spelled incorrectly

16. Which of the following steps in assembly language operation would occur FIRST?

    A. Translation into machine language
    B. Passage of instructions through link editor
    C. Writing source program
    D. Output of object program

17. In machine language, the symbol for a displacement value is

    A. X
    B. Y
    C. Z
    D. A

18. In an assembly language, the place at which computer control can be transferred is marked by the

    A. operand field
    B. label field
    C. operation code
    D. register number

19. The purpose of a data address is to

    A. signify which register to use when computational procedures are required
    B. tell the control unit what data-processing operation is to be performed
    C. construct a base register for each instruction
    D. locate elements in the computer's primary memory

20. Which of the following is a fourth-generation programming language?

    A. IFPS   B. FORTRAN   C. RPG   D. ADA

21. _____ is represented by the program flowchart symbol shown below.

    A. Preparation
    B. Processing
    C. Decision
    D. Terminal

22. Each of the following is an advantage associated with the use of HIPO charts EXCEPT

    A. designs programs in testable models
    B. creation of hierarchy of detail as design progresses
    C. places highest priority on means
    D. clear indication of necessary inputs and outputs

23. Which of the following is NOT a disadvantage associated with the use of BASIC?

    A. Minimal language standards
    B. Developed after FORTRAN
    C. Not self-documenting
    D. Easily combined syntax errors

24. A group of instructions within a computer program that performs a specific function is known as a(n)

    A. subroutine
    B. drone
    C. loop
    D. processor

25. Each of the following is a debugging aid that helps identify logic errors in a program EXCEPT

    A. control totals
    B. diagnostic error message
    C. control breaks
    D. trace routines

KEY (CORRECT ANSWERS)

1. B	11. D
2. D	12. A
3. A	13. A
4. B	14. C
5. D	15. B
6. B	16. C
7. B	17. C
8. C	18. B
9. D	19. D
10. B	20. A

21. C
22. C
23. D
24. A
25. B

EXAMINATION SECTION
TEST 1

DIRECTIONS: Each question or incomplete statement is followed by several suggested answers or completions. Select the one that BEST answers the question or completes the statement. *PRINT THE LETTER OF THE CORRECT ANSWER IN THE SPACE AT THE RIGHT.*

1. A form such as a sales invoice is called a(n) _____ document.

    A. audit
    B. original
    C. source
    D. input
    E. machine-readable

    1._____

2. A complete computer system will consist of people, procedures, hardware, software and

    A. tasks
    B. data
    C. input/output devices
    D. programs
    E. all of the above

    2._____

3. The person responsible for programming applications such as payroll, inventory, accounts receivable, etc. is the

    A. systems programmer
    B. lead programmer
    C. applications programmer
    D. computer analyst
    E. computer operator

    3._____

4. A documented record of transactions through the entire processing cycle is called a(n)

    A. transaction log
    B. source document
    C. object document
    D. audit trail
    E. control tape

    4._____

5. Which of the following BEST describes the steps involved in completing a project by a computer systems analyst?

    A. Problem analysis, problem design, coding, testing, debugging
    B. Flowcharting, coding, testing
    C. System design, testing, maintenance
    D. Preliminary investigation, detailed investigation, system design, system development, system implementation and evaluation, system maintenance
    E. Detailed investigation, reports to management, programming, installation, testing

    5._____

6. When initially collecting data to conduct a systems project, the computer system analyst should collect data from people via

    A. multiple choice questionnaires
    B. fill-in the blank questionnaires
    C. open-ended questionnaires
    D. observing their work habits
    E. personal interviews

    6._____

7. The MOST commonly used tool by analysts today to graphically illustrate the flow of data through a system is by

    A. flowcharts
    B. Warnier-Orr diagrams
    C. Gantt Charts
    D. the Nassi-Schneiderman Chart
    E. data flow diagrams

8. Of input, output, processing, storage methods, and procedures, the one designed first by the analyst is

    A. input
    B. output
    C. processing
    D. storage methods
    E. procedures

9. A list and description of all of the data elements required in a system is listed in a(n)

    A. audit trail
    B. compilation listing
    C. data dictionary
    D. transaction journal
    E. system documentation

10. System controls are instituted to

    A. prevent computer fraud
    B. ensure valid input of data
    C. ensure that reports contain valid information
    D. ensure data is processed completely and accurately
    E. all of the above

11. A method used by the analyst to document the scheduling of the completion of a project is a(n)

    A. flowchart
    B. hierarchy chart
    C. Gantt chart
    D. Warnier-Orr diagram
    E. data flow diagram

12. A method of converting a manual system to an automated system whereby both systems are run simultaneously, whereupon the results are compared and the new system is phased in, is called _____ conversion.

    A. parallel
    B. test-site
    C. direct
    D. concurrent
    E. hybrid

13. The MOST important skill or requirement of the analyst is

    A. good communication skills
    B. proper academic background
    C. good programming skills
    D. good management skills
    E. technical expertise

14. If the analyst fails to consult with the payroll department before developing a new payroll system, the analyst failed to follow the guideline of

    A. developing a structured system
    B. developing a *top-down* system
    C. developing a system with the end-user's needs being of paramount importance
    D. providing for future expansion and change
    E. all of the above

15. In most cases, a request for computer services should originate from

    A. the computer analyst's department
    B. upper level management
    C. the users of the requested system
    D. lower management
    E. mid-management

16. The records contained in the _____ file are *usually* created from source documents. They are later read in to update other, more permanent files

    A. master   B. detail   C. summary
    D. transaction   E. temporary

17. The device which is MOST commonly used for input into the computer system is the

    A. tape drive   B. printer
    C. video terminal   D. optical disk reader
    E. disk drive

18. The process whereby an analyst compares the expenses against the advantages of a computerized system is called

    A. RFP   B. detailed analysis
    C. cost/benefit analysis   D. conversion costing
    E. none of the above

19. Most business computer applications are written in which of the following computer languages?

    A. BASIC   B. RPG   C. C
    D. FORTRAN   E. None of the above

20. When gathering facts to study the procedures and transactions of a system, the analyst should consult

    A. management
    B. users
    C. existing documentation
    D. other members of the computer staff
    E. all of the above

21. Which analysis and design tool used by the computer system analyst shows the levels and subdivisions of a computer system?

    A. Data flow diagram   B. System flowchart
    C. Hierarchy chart   D. Pseudocode
    E. Decision table

22. During the design of input, the analyst establishes

    A. format and layout of reports
    B. how to store data
    C. how to collect data
    D. methods of processing input data
    E. which data is needed by users

23. The analyst establishes systems controls. The purpose of these controls is to detect

    A. computer hardware errors
    B. computer software flaws
    C. data entry errors
    D. errors on printed reports
    E. all of the above

24. The MOST commonly used tool that the analyst uses to design printed output reports is the

    A. video display layout
    B. VTOC
    C. data dictionary
    D. printer layout form
    E. flowchart template

25. In respect to the use of microcomputers, the problem of MOST concern to the systems analyst is the

    A. lack of user friendly software
    B. lack of communications ability with mainframe computers
    C. lack of operating systems
    D. lack of standardization
    E. high cost

KEY (CORRECT ANSWERS)

1. C
2. B
3. C
4. D
5. D

6. E
7. E
8. B
9. C
10. E

11. C
12. A
13. A
14. E
15. C

16. D
17. C
18. C
19. E
20. E

21. C
22. C
23. E
24. D
25. D

TEST 2

DIRECTIONS: Each question or incomplete statement is followed by several suggested answers or completions. Select the one that *BEST* answers the question or completes the statement. *PRINT THE LETTER OF THE CORRECT ANSWER IN THE SPACE AT THE RIGHT.*

1. A type of output document that is also used as an input document is called a _____ document. 1.__

    A. source B. turnaround C. master
    D. transaction E. detail

2. The _____ report reveals all data for every single transaction. 2.__

    A. master B. transaction C. summary
    D. detail E. exception

3. A 9 placed on a report design form is used to indicate 3.__

    A. numeric data B. alphabetic data
    C. quantity data D. page numbering
    E. non-numeric data

4. A Z placed on a report design form is used to indicate 4.__

    A. numeric data B. alphabetic data
    C. zero suppression D. a date
    E. non-numeric edited item

5. An X on a report design form is used to indicate 5.__

    A. alphanumeric data B. zero suppression
    C. page numbering D. numeric data
    E. numbers to be printed as currency

6. The totaling of specific rows and/or columns in a report is called 6.__

    A. auditing B. summarizing
    C. crossfooting D. detailing
    E. control totals

7. A temporary data file is called a _____ file. 7.__

    A. transaction B. scratch C. master
    D. detail E. backup

8. Which type of media has been MOST commonly used for backup files? 8.__

    A. Floppy disk B. Disk cartridges
    C. Video cards D. Magnetic tape
    E. Optical disks

9. The media BEST suited for on-line processing is(are) 9.__

    A. magnetic disk B. magnetic tape
    C. video cards D. magnetic drum
    E. all of the above

64

10. An advantage of a Data Base Management System is 10._____

    A. data integrity
    B. reduced data redundancy
    C. consolidation of files
    D. easier access to data
    E. all of the above

11. A type of Data Base Management System where data is *linked* together via a common data field is called a _____ database. 11._____

    A. hierarchial
    B. network
    C. Boyce-Codd
    D. relational
    E. flat file

12. The type of input data validation test that checks for an error in the placement of a decimal point is the _____ test. 12._____

    A. batch total
    B. crossfooting
    C. slide
    D. control total
    E. transposition

13. The system analyst may solicit hardware and software proposals from vendors. The analyst will do so by preparing this document. 13._____

    A. RFQ   B. RFP   C. RJE   D. TOS   E. OCR

14. This computer language was originally endorsed as the *primary* language to be used on projects authorized by the Department of Defense. 14._____

    A. Ada
    B. COBOL
    C. FORTRAN
    D. C
    E. BASIC

15. Which tool is used by the analyst to schedule when and how long an activity should take place to complete a project? 15._____

    A. PERT chart
    B. VTOC
    C. HIPO chart
    D. Data dictionary
    E. Data flow diagram

16. Program testing is carried out by computer 16._____

    A. analysts
    B. programmers
    C. operators
    D. management
    E. users

17. Which group makes the final decision whether or not a system will be implemented? 17._____

    A. management
    B. users
    C. system analysts
    D. programmers
    E. operators

18. Which type of accounting system tracks money owed to a company or organization by clients or customers? 18._____

    A. Accounts payable
    B. General ledger
    C. Payroll
    D. Inventory
    E. Accounts receivable

19. Which type of accounting system keeps track of descriptions, reorder points, quantities, costs, and vendors of items on hand?

    A. General ledger
    B. Inventory
    C. Payroll
    D. Accounts receivable
    E. Accounts payable

20. A chronological listing of financial transactions is called a

    A. general journal
    B. general ledger
    C. debits and credits
    D. transaction log
    E. audit trail

21. Automating the inventory control system to include reordering inventory might be in violation of which of the following guideline(s)?

    A. Develop systems that are independent of the organization
    B. Integrate systems but avoid complexity
    C. Determine the proper level of automation
    D. Automate routine, repetitive functions
    E. All of the above

22. A virtual system

    A. requires that programs be written so that they conform to memory size limitations
    B. places an entire software application into memory as it is executed
    C. requires that the programmer divide programs into modules or segments
    D. has methods of dividing programs into pages or segments that are loaded into memory as needed
    E. allows multiple programs to be executed at the same time

23. When a systems analyst solicits hardware and/or software from an outside vendor, the analyst should select the hardware and/or software that

    A. exceeds the minimum operating requirements
    B. meets the organization's needs and is competitively priced
    C. meets the organization's budget
    D. can be delivered on time
    E. is from a major manufacturer of the type of product requested

24. Analysts often gather information through the use of questionnaires. A type of questionnaire which uses very explicit questions and requires a short, written response is called a(n) _____ questionnaire.

    A. open ended
    B. multiple choice
    C. direct response
    D. true/false
    E. closed questions

25. During the preliminary investigation, the analyst will gather information

    A. by interviewing top-level management
    B. from all users, using questionnaires
    C. by reviewing all documentation of the existing system
    D. through time and motion studies, observations and interviews
    E. all of the above

KEY (CORRECT ANSWERS)

1.	B	11.	D
2.	D	12.	C
3.	A	13.	B
4.	C	14.	A
5.	A	15.	A
6.	C	16.	B
7.	B	17.	A
8.	D	18.	E
9.	A	19.	B
10.	E	20.	A

21. C
22. D
23. B
24. C
25. A

EXAMINATION SECTION
TEST 1

DIRECTIONS: Each question or incomplete statement is followed by several suggested answers or completions. Select the one that BEST answers the question or completes the statement. *PRINT THE LETTER OF THE CORRECT ANSWER IN THE SPACE AT THE RIGHT.*

1. The stage in a system's life cycle in which logical and physical specifications are produced is called

    A. implementation
    B. design
    C. conception
    D. documentation

2. Which of the following is a network topology that links a number of computers by a single circuit with all messages broadcast to the entire network?

    A. Daisy-chain
    B. Broadband
    C. Bus
    D. Ring

3. Of the following statements about information as a resource, which is generally FALSE?

    A. It has value and lends itself to the process of management.
    B. It can be overabundant and overused.
    C. Its usefulness tends to decrease with time.
    D. It can be consumed and expended in the same way as many capital resources.

4. What is the term for the extra bit built into EBCDIC and ASCII codes that is used as a check bit to insure accuracy?

    A. Parity   B. Auditor   C. Damper   D. Buffer

5. In the systems development process, which of the following is typically performed FIRST?

    A. Conversion
    B. Programming
    C. Production
    D. Testing

6. Which of the following is a term for a device used to store and retrieve large numbers of optical disks?

    A. Warehouse   B. Vault   C. Clearing   D. Jukebox

7. Each of the following can generally be said to be an element of the changing contemporary business environment EXCEPT

    A. global work groups
    B. stable environment
    C. location independence
    D. time-based competition

8. Of the following methods of changing from one information system to another, which is generally considered to be the safest?

    A. Pilot study
    B. Direct cutover
    C. Phased approach
    D. Parallel strategy

9. Which of the following is NOT typically a characteristic of a management information system?

   A. Extensive analytical capability
   B. Known and stable information requirements
   C. Internal rather than external orientation
   D. Generally reporting–and control–oriented

10. In information systems terminology, a person, place, or thing about which information must be kept is referred to as a(n)

    A. element
    B. entity
    C. assemblage
    D. pixel

11. Which of the following are considered to be moral dimensions that are emblematic of the information age?
    I. Accountability and control
    II. Property rights
    III. Quality of life
    IV. Information rights and obligations

    The CORRECT answer is:

    A. I, II
    B. I, II, III
    C. I, III, IV
    D. I, II, III, IV

12. In order to be classified as a *mainframe,* a computer must typically have at LEAST

    A. 1 remote access server
    B. 50 megabytes of RAM
    C. 1 gigabyte of RAM
    D. 5 gigabytes of secondary storage space

13. For most organizations, the FIRST step in developing a telecommunications plan should be to

    A. identify critical areas where telecommunications currently has an impact
    B. identify the organization's long–range business plan
    C. identify critical areas where telecommunications may have a future impact
    D. audit existing telecommunications functions

14. What is the term for a change in a data signal, from positive to negative or vice–versa, that is used as a measure of transmission speed?

    A. Baud
    B. Switch
    C. Byte
    D. Bit

15. Currently, in service industries such as finance, insurance, and real estate, information technology generally constitutes about _____% of invested capital.

    A. 10
    B. 30
    C. 50
    D. 70

16. Which of the following signifies the emerging standard language for relational database management systems?

    A. SGML
    B. HTML
    C. Perl
    D. SQL

17. Over time, organizations have developed an ethical framework for handling system-related issues. Generally, the first step in any organization's ethical analysis should be to identify

   A. the higher-order values involved
   B. the potential consequences of any decision
   C. reasonable options
   D. the stakeholders

18. Telephone lines that are continously available for transmission by a lessee are described as

   A. validated
   B. denuded
   C. formalized
   D. dedicated

19. In a typical telecommunications system, a message that originates from the host computer will then pass through a

   A. front-end processor
   B. modem
   C. controller
   D. multiplexer

20. The table or list that relates record keys to physical locations on direct access files is called the

   A. key
   B. index
   C. card file
   D. criterion

21. Which of the following offers the best definition of *data* as it applies to information systems?

   A. Things that are known to have occurred, to exist, or to be true
   B. Productions of exact copies of documents by electronic scanning and transmission
   C. Information not previously known to people within an organization
   D. Raw facts that have not been organized and arranged into understandable and usable form

22. A logical unit of a program that performs one or a small number of functions is known as a(n)

   A. module
   B. element
   C. loop
   D. packet

23. Which of the following is a fourth-generation computer language?

   A. FORTRAN
   B. dBASE
   C. C
   D. Ada

24. The logical description of an entire database, listing all the data elements and the relationships among them, is known as the

   A. value chain
   B. schema
   C. matrix
   D. shell

25. Systems theory defines a system as an entity that is generally greater than the sum of its parts. Which of the following terms describes this condition?

   A. Synchronicity
   B. Collectivism
   C. Interdependence
   D. Synergy

KEY (CORRECT ANSWERS)

1. B
2. C
3. D
4. A
5. D

6. D
7. B
8. D
9. A
10. B

11. D
12. B
13. D
14. A
15. D

16. D
17. A
18. D
19. A
20. B

21. D
22. A
23. B
24. B
25. D

———

TEST 2

DIRECTIONS: Each question or incomplete statement is followed by several suggested answers or completions. Select the one that BEST answers the question or completes the statement. *PRINT THE LETTER OF THE CORRECT ANSWER IN THE SPACE AT THE RIGHT.*

1. Of the types of organizational change that are enabled by information technology, which involves the highest levels of risk and reward?

    A. Paradigm shift
    B. Automation
    C. Business reengineering
    D. Rationalization of procedures

2. Most local–area networks (LANS) are _____ networks.

    A. token ring   B. ring   C. star   D. bus

3. Which of the following is an input device which translates images into digital form for processing?

    A. Surveyor   B. Pen   C. Compiler   D. Scanner

4. In a system, the appearance of an additional pattern or sequence of states is referred to as

    A. autonomy
    B. differentiation
    C. bifurcation
    D. variation

5. Which of the following is NOT considered to be an information output?

    A. Storage
    B. Expert–system advice
    C. Query response
    D. Report

6. Which of the following is a direct access storage device (DASD)?

    A. Punch card
    B. Sequential tape
    C. Printed page
    D. Magnetic disk

7. Which of the following is most likely to be an output from a knowledge work system (KWS)?

    A. Special report
    B. Model
    C. Summary report
    D. Query response

8. A system resting on accepted and fixed definitions of data and procedures, operating with predefined rules, is described in systems terminology as

    A. formal
    B. computer–based
    C. fixed
    D. expert

9. Which of the following is a characteristic of operational data? They

    A. are stored on a single platform
    B. contain recent as well as historical data
    C. are organized around major business informational subjects
    D. are generally used by isolated legacy systems

10. Which of the following signifies a telecommunications network that requires its own dedicated channels and encompasses a limited physical distance?

    A. WAN   B. KWS   C. LAN   D. ISDN

11. Which of the following terms is used for the capture or collection of raw data from within the organization, or from its external environment, for processing in an information system?

    A. Feedback   B. Tracking   C. Entry   D. Input

12. What is the term for the high-speed storage of frequently used instructions and data?

    A. Cache   B. Index   C. Reserve   D. Packet

13. Which of the following represents the largest unit of data?

    A. Byte   B. Record   C. Field   D. File

14. In most organizations, the entire system-building effort is driven by

    A. user information requirements
    B. existing hardware
    C. user training requirements
    D. availability of packaged applications

15. Which of the following terms is used to describe a process of change governed by probabilities at each step?

    A. Adiabatic   B. Stochastic
    C. Multifinal   D. Probabilistic

16. In object-oriented programming, a specific class of objects often receives the features of a more general class. This process is referred to as

    A. aliasing   B. inheritance
    C. summation   D. incrementation

17. In a typical organization, the strategic planning of an MIS would be the responsibility of the

    A. steering committee
    B. project teams
    C. operations personnel and end users
    D. chief information officer

18. Which of the following is a specialized computer that supervises communications traffic between the CPU and the peripheral devices in a telecommunications system?

    A. Controller   B. Concentrator
    C. Connector   D. Compiler

19. Of the following steps in the machine cycle of a computer, which occurs FIRST?

    A. Transmission of data from main memory to storage register
    B. Placement of instruction in instruction register
    C. ALU performance
    D. Placement of instruction in address register

20. Which of the following is a process of recoding information which reduces the number of different characters in a message while increasing the different number of characters to be recognized?

    A. The black box method   B. Daisy chaining
    C. Aliasing   D. Chunking

21. Of the following methodologies for establishing organizational MIS requirements, which is most explicitly oriented toward deploying information systems as a competitive weapon?

    A. Critical success factors (CSF)
    B. Strategic cube and value chain
    C. Business sytems planning (BSP)
    D. Strategy set transformation

22. Which of the following is a type of MIS application used for tracking and monitoring?

    A. Database
    B. Decision Support System (DSS)
    C. Spreadsheet
    D. Desktop publishing

23. An organization's information requirements are often analyzed by looking at the entire organization in terms of units, functions, processes, and data elements. What is the term most frequently used for such an examination?

    A. Semantic networking   B. Decision support
    C. Enterprise analysis   D. Run control

24. Which of the following would most likely be classifed as an *information worker*?

    A. Engineer   B. Scientist
    C. Data processor   D. Architect

25. In an organization that uses a decision support system to make stock investment decisions, which of the following would be classified as memory aids to the system?

    A. Graphs   B. Databases
    C. Menus   D. Training documents

KEY (CORRECT ANSWERS)

1. A
2. D
3. D
4. C
5. A

6. D
7. B
8. A
9. D
10. C

11. D
12. A
13. D
14. A
15. B

16. B
17. D
18. A
19. B
20. D

21. B
22. A
23. C
24. C
25. B

TEST 3

DIRECTIONS: Each question or incomplete statement is followed by several suggested answers or completions. Select the one that BEST answers the question or completes the statement. *PRINT THE LETTER OF THE CORRECT ANSWER IN THE SPACE AT THE RIGHT.*

1. In the _____ process, the components of a system and their relationship to each other are laid out as they would appear to users.

    A. external integration
    B. logical design
    C. file serving
    D. hierarchical

    1.____

2. Over the past two decades, technological trends have raised ethical issues in society, especially in the area of privacy. Which of the following trends has LEAST directly impacted the issue of privacy?

    A. Advances in data storage techniques and declining storage costs
    B. Advances in telecommunications infrastructure
    C. The doubling of computer power every 18 months
    D. Advances in data mining techniques for large databases

    2.____

3. Which of the following systems exists at the strategic level of an organization?

    A. Expert system
    B. Decision support system (DSS)
    C. Value chain
    D. Executive support system (ESS)

    3.____

4. Which of the following is equal to one–billionth of a second?

    A. Millisecond
    B. Picosecond
    C. Nanosecond
    D. Microsecond

    4.____

5. A small section of a program that can be easily stored in primary storage and quickly accessed from secondary storage is a(n)

    A. sector   B. module   C. page   D. applet

    5.____

6. Which of the following statements about hierarchical and network database systems is TRUE?
    They

    A. do support English–language inquiries for information
    B. involve easily changeable access pathways
    C. are difficult to install
    D. are relatively inefficient processors

    6.____

7. Which of the following is a programming language that is portable across different brands of soft hardware, and is used for both military and nonmilitary applications?

    A. FORTRAN   B. Pascal   C. Ada   D. C

    7.____

8. Which of the following would be LEAST likely to be an output of an office automation system (OAS)?

    A. Memo   B. Schedule   C. List   D. Mail

    8.____

77

9. At a minimum, an information system must consist of all of the following EXCEPT

   A. computers B. data C. people D. procedures

10. What is the term for the strategy used to search through the rule base in an expert system?

    A. Index server
    B. Key field
    C. Register
    D. Inference engine

11. Which of the following communications media has the greatest frequency range?

    A. Wireless (electromagnetic)
    B. Fiber optics
    C. Wireless (PCS)
    D. Microwave

12. Models of decision–making in which decisions are shaped by the organization's standard operation procedures are described as

    A. systems–oriented
    B. indexed
    C. bureaucratic
    D. sequential

13. The first element involved in a standard dataflow diagram is a(n)

    A. dataflow
    B. external entity
    C. data store
    D. process

14. A system that seeks a set of related goals is described as

    A. purposive B. closed C. fixed D. driven

15. Weaknesses in a system's _____ controls may affect the entire system of general controls, which may not be properly executed or enforced.

    A. administrative
    B. software
    C. implementation
    D. computer operations

16. Current and historical data from operational systems is often consolidated for management reporting and analysis into a database with reporting and query tools. This type of database is usually referred to as a(n)

    A. warehouse
    B. redundancy
    C. controller
    D. library

17. A project manager at an organization plans to compose letters outlining details of an upcoming trade show to be addressed individually to several dozen employees. The most appropriate type of application for this purpose is

    A. simple word processing
    B. desktop publishing
    C. a mail merge
    D. an automated document

18. In the process of systems analysis, which of the following procedures is typically performed FIRST?

    A. Defining a problem that can be solved by a newly designed system
    B. Examining existing documents
    C. Identifying the primary owners and users of data in the organization
    D. Identifying the information requirements that must be met by a system solution

19. Each of the following is a method for performing a data quality audit EXCEPT surveying

    A. data dictionaries
    B. entire data files
    C. end users for perceptions of data quality
    D. samples from data files

20. Which of the following signifies semiconductor memory chips that contain program instructions?

    A. RAM   B. ROM   C. CPU   D. ALU

21. The Fair Information Practices Principles set forth in 1973 include:
    I. Individuals have rights of access, inspection, review, and amendment to systems that contain information about them
    II. Managers of systems are responsible and can be held liable for the damages done by systems, for the reliability, and for their security
    III. Managers do not have the right of access to any form of interorganizational correspondence if individuals do not wish to grant such access
    IV. Governments have the right to intervene in the information relationships among private parties

    The CORRECT answer is:

    A. I, II
    B. II, III
    C. I, II, IV
    D. II, III, IV

22. In information systems terminology, a group of records of the same type is known as a

    A. class   B. field   C. batch   D. file

23. In systems theory, communication which travels through informal rather than formal channels is known as

    A. noise
    B. back channel communication
    C. cross–talk
    D. the grapevine

24. In order to be useful as a resource, information must satisfy each of the following conditions EXCEPT it must

    A. be accurate
    B. be available when needed
    C. reinforce beliefs
    D. relate to the business or matters at hand

25. In most contemporary organizations, the role of an MIS department can be described as   25._____
    A. performing key design and analysis functions, before and after a systems design has been implemented
    B. designing, installing, testing, and maintaining all organizational computer–based information and communications systems
    C. providing and perfecting all information and communications needs at the organization's management level
    D. coordinating corporate MIS efforts and providing an overall computational infrastructure

---

KEY (CORRECT ANSWERS)

1.	B	11.	C
2.	C	12.	C
3.	D	13.	B
4.	C	14.	A
5.	C	15.	A
6.	C	16.	A
7.	C	17.	C
8.	C	18.	C
9.	A	19.	A
10.	D	20.	B

21. C
22. D
23. B
24. C
25. D

EXAMINATION SECTION
TEST 1

DIRECTIONS: Each question or incomplete statement is followed by several suggested answers or completions. Select the one that BEST answers the question or completes the statement. *PRINT THE LETTER OF THE CORRECT ANSWER IN THE SPACE AT THE RIGHT.*

1. A microprocessor includes media for each of the following EXCEPT

    A. secondary storage B. control
    C. logic D. memory

2. Which of the following protocols is LEAST likely to be used in a wide-area network (WAN)?

    A. SNA B. Token passing
    C. TCP/IP D. DEC DNA

3. In an expert system, the rule base is sometimes searched using a strategy that begins with a hypothesis and seeks out more information until the hypothesis is either proved or disproved. This strategy is known as

    A. backward chaining
    B. key fielding
    C. indexed sequential access
    D. process specification

4. The meaning of signs, symbols, messages or systems are involved in a body of inquiry known as

    A. linguistics B. semantics
    C. communications D. syntactics

5. Which of the following is a query language?

    A. Nomad B. Ideal C. Systat D. RPG-III

6. Which of the following is the typical unit of measurement used by systems designers to estimate the length of time needed to complete a project?

    A. Data-week B. Man-hour
    C. File-hour D. Man-month

7. Which of the following is the oldest professional computer society in the United States?

    A. Data Processing Management Association (DPMA)
    B. Institute for Certification of Computer Professionals (ICP)
    C. Association of Computing Machinery (ACM)
    D. Information Technology Association of America (ITAA)

8. Which of the following terms is commonly used to describe the interaction of people and machines in the work environment, especially in terms of job design and health issues?

    A. Connectivity B. Ergonomics
    C. Feasibility D. Interface

9. Which of the following is a likely application of the sensitivity analysis models of a decision-support system?

    A. Forecasting sales
    B. Determining the proper product mix within a given market
    C. Predicting the actions of competitors
    D. Goal seeking

10. What is the term for the temporary storage location in a control unit where small amounts of data or instructions reside for thousandths of a second just before use?

    A. Cache   B. Register   C. Sector   D. Buffer

11. Systems whose behavior includes options without specification of probabilities within the system are described as

    A. runaway   B. possibilistic
    C. stochastic   D. probabilistic

12. The physical devices and software that link various hardware components and transfer data from one physical location to another are known collectively as

    A. cyberspace
    B. wide-area networks
    C. telecommunications technology
    D. semantic networks

13. Which of the following is a tangible benefit associated with organizational information systems?

    A. Streamlined operations   B. Higher asset utilization
    C. Inventory reduction   D. Improved planning

14. Which of the following is NOT generally considered to be a physical component of an MIS?

    A. Personnel   B. Information
    C. Procedures   D. Software

15. Any undesired information in a communication channel which is not part of the intended message is typically referred to as

    A. resistance   B. noise
    C. data error   D. cross-talk

16. Which of the following is the ASCII 8-bit binary code for the number 1?

    A. 0001 0001   B. 0101 0001
    C. 0000 1000   D. 1001 0001

17. Which of the following is a method of organizing expert system knowledge into chunks in which relationships are based on shared characteristics determined by the user?

    A. Indexing   B. GUI
    C. Batch processing   D. Frames

18. Which of the following is a telecommunications requirement that is particular to the task of on–line data entry?

   A. High–capacity video and data capabilities
   B. Infrequent, high–volume bursts of information
   C. Instant response
   D. Direct response

19. What is the term for the technology which breaks blocks of text into small fixed bundles of data and routes them in an economical way through an available communications channel?

   A. Optical character recognition
   B. Frame relay
   C. Packet switching
   D. Branch exchange

20. A transaction processing system rejects a transaction on the basis that it includes a Social Security number which contains an alphabetic character. This is an example of a(n) _____ check.

   A. reasonableness
   B. format
   C. dependency
   D. existence

21. The smallest unit of data for defining an image in a computer is the

   A. byte   B. pixel   C. quark   D. bit

22. In a microcomputer, which of the following transmits signals specifying whether to read or write data from a given primary storage address, input device, or output device?

   A. Control bus
   B. Address bus
   C. Data bus
   D. CPU

23. Which of the following stages occurs the LATEST in the traditional systems life cycle model?

   A. Systems study
   B. Programming
   C. Design
   D. Project definition

24. The fastest and most expensive memory used in a microcomputer is located in the

   A. cache   B. register   C. hard disk   D. RAM

25. Which of the following is an optical disk system that allows users to record data only once, but to read the data indefinitely?

   A. WORM   B. EPROM   C. RAM   D. TQM

KEY (CORRECT ANSWERS)

1.	A	11.	B
2.	B	12.	C
3.	A	13.	C
4.	B	14.	B
5.	D	15.	B
6.	D	16.	B
7.	C	17.	D
8.	B	18.	D
9.	D	19.	C
10.	B	20.	B

21. B
22. A
23. B
24. B
25. A

TEST 2

DIRECTIONS: Each question or incomplete statement is followed by several suggested answers or completions. Select the one that BEST answers the question or completes the statement. *PRINT THE LETTER OF THE CORRECT ANSWER IN THE SPACE AT THE RIGHT.*

1. Which of the following styles of systems development is most often used for information systems at the individual level?

    A. End–user computing
    B. Commercial software packages
    C. Prototyping
    D. Traditional life cycle

2. Which of the following is a programming language that was developed in 1956 for scientific and mathematical applications?

    A. COBOL   B. BASIC   C. Pascal   D. FORTRAN

3. Which of the following personnel would be considered a *technical specialist* in an MIS department?

    A. Education specialist   B. Database administrator
    C. Applications programmer   D. Systems analyst

4. Which of the following is NOT a characteristic of a fault–tolerant system?

    A. The use of special software routines to detect hardware failures
    B. Extra memory chips, processors, and disk storage
    C. Continuous detection of bugs or program defects
    D. Hardware parts that can be removed without system disruption

5. Defining a system program in such a way that it may call itself is an example of

    A. eudemony   B. recursion
    C. redundancy   D. artificial intelligence

6. What is the term used to enumerate the number of bits that can be processed at one time by a computer?

    A. Data bus width   B. Word length
    C. RAM capacity   D. Bandwidth

7. Which of the following is another term for a field, or a grouping of characters into a word, group of words, or complete number?

    A. Code   B. Byte
    C. Data element   D. File

8. A person in a multi–user system sends a message using the OSI model to another user at a different location. At the messenger's end of the system, after passing through the *session* layer of the model, the message will then enter the _____ layer.

    A. transport   B. network
    C. presentation   D. data link

9. Which of the following is NOT a disadvantage associated with the traditional life cycle model of systems development?

   A. Time consumption
   B. Oversimplification
   C. Cost
   D. Inflexibility

10. Transmission speeds that would fall within the expected range of coaxial cable are _____ per second.

    A. 400 bits
    B. 50 megabits
    C. 300 megabits
    D. 7 gigabits

11. Which of the following is a telecommunications computer that collects and temporarily stores messages from terminals for batch transmission to the host computer?

    A. Assembler
    B. Concentrator
    C. Buffer
    D. Compiler

12. Which of the following is an advantage associated with the centralized or teleprocessing model of multi-user systems?

    A. Local computing
    B. Scaleability
    C. Low start-up costs
    D. Low technical risk

13. Software systems that can operate on different hardware platforms are referred to as _____ systems.

    A. open
    B. interoperable
    C. branched
    D. transmigrational

14. What is the term for the process by which the properties of a collection (i.e., of data) are described in terms of the sums of the properties of the units contained in the collection?

    A. Unity
    B. Autarky
    C. Chunking
    D. Aggregation

15. In systems terminology, what is the term for output that is returned to the appropriate members of an organization to help them evaluate or correct input?

    A. Exit data
    B. Feedback
    C. Assessor
    D. Valuation

16. The years 1957 to 1963 are generally considered to have been the _____ generation in the evolution of computer hardware technology.

    A. first
    B. second
    C. third
    D. fourth

17. A conversion approach in which the new system completely replaces the old one on an appointed day is known as

    A. focused differentiation
    B. direct cutover
    C. allied distribution
    D. batch processing

18. Of the following types of business network redesign, the one that can be said to be most highly coupled is/are

    A. interenterprise system access
    B. knowledge networks
    C. EDI
    D. interenterprise process integration

19. Which of the following terms is used to describe the shape or configuration of a telecommunications network?

    A. Duplex
    B. Topology
    C. Protocol
    D. Transmissivity

20. Which of the following is/are recognized differences between microcomputers and workstations?
    I. Microcomputers have more powerful mathematical processing capabilities.
    II. Microcomputers are more useful for computer–aided design (CAD).
    III. Workstations are more widely used by knowledge workers.
    IV. Workstations can more easily perform multiple tasks simultaneously.

    The CORRECT answer is:

    A. I, II   B. II, III   C. III, IV   D. II, IV

21. Which of the following signifies a tool for retrieving and transferring files from a remote computer?

    A. EDI   B. CPU   C. TCP/IP   D. FTP

22. Which of the following is a federal privacy law that applies to private institutions?

    A. Freedom of Information Act of 1968 (as amended)
    B. Privacy Act of 1974 (as amended)
    C. Privacy Protection Act of 1980
    D. Computer Matching and Privacy Protection Act of 1988

23. The main contribution of end–user systems development typically occurs in the area of

    A. productivity enhancement
    B. improved updating functions
    C. increased technical complexity
    D. improved efficiency in transaction processing

24. In cooperative processing, a mainframe and a microcomputer generally share tasks. The mainframe, however, is generally best at performing

    A. screen presentation
    B. error processing
    C. data field editing
    D. file input and output

25. In a systems development process, users are made active members of development project teams, and some users are placed in charge of system training and installation. In this case, management has made use of _____ tools.

    A. external integration   B. internal integration
    C. formal planning   D. formal control

25.___

KEY (CORRECT ANSWERS)

1. C
2. D
3. B
4. C
5. B

6. B
7. C
8. A
9. B
10. B

11. B
12. D
13. A
14. D
15. B

16. B
17. B
18. B
19. B
20. C

21. D
22. C
23. A
24. D
25. A

TEST 3

DIRECTIONS: Each question or incomplete statement is followed by several suggested answers or completions. Select the one that BEST answers the question or completes the statement. *PRINT THE LETTER OF THE CORRECT ANSWER IN THE SPACE AT THE RIGHT.*

1. As a general rule, the development of a system that will be used by others can be expected to take_____ as long as the development of an individual system that will be used only by the developer.

    A. half
    B. twice
    C. three times
    D. five times

    1.____

2. In LANs, the token ring configuration is most useful for

    A. broadcasting messages to the entire network through a single circuit
    B. multidirectional transmissions between microcomputers or between micros and a larger computer
    C. transmissions between microcomputers and a larger computer that require a degree of traffic control
    D. transmitting large volumes of data between microcomputers

    2.____

3. Which of the following statements about expert systems is generally TRUE? They

    A. function best in lower–level clerical functions
    B. require minimal development resources
    C. are highly adaptable over time
    D. are capable of representing a wide range of causal models

    3.____

4. A middle-range machine with a RAM capacity that measures from about 10 megabytes to over 1 gigabyte is known as a

    A. microcomputer
    B. minicomputer
    C. desktop computer
    D. mainframe

    4.____

5. Which of the following media uses the sector method for storing data?

    A. Cache
    B. Floppy disk
    C. Hard disk
    D. CD–ROM

    5.____

6. When mechanisms of functional subsystems are connected causally to influence each other, they are said to be

    A. aggregated
    B. coupled
    C. synchronous
    D. constrained

    6.____

7. Which of the following storage media generally has the largest capacity?

    A. Cache
    B. Magnetic disk
    C. Optical disk
    D. Magnetic tape

    7.____

8. In terms of information ethics, the mechanisms for assessing responsibility for decisions and actions are referred to as

    A. liability
    B. capacity
    C. creditability
    D. accountability

    8.____

9. Which of the following signifies the central switching system that handles a firm's voice and digital communications?

   A. OSI   B. DSS   C. PBX   D. LAN

10. What is the term for the LAN channel technology that provides a single path for transmitting text, graphics, voice, or video data at one time?

    A. Bus
    C. Firewall
    B. Baseband
    D. Broadband

11. The stage in a system's life cycle in which testing, training, and conversion occur is termed

    A. evaluation
    C. installation
    B. design
    D. documentation

12. Which of the following is NOT a type of processor used in telecommunications systems?

    A. Coaxial cable
    C. Modem
    B. Controller
    D. Multiplexer

13. A database that is stored in more than one physical location is described as

    A. sequential
    C. distributed
    B. wide-area
    D. indexed

14. An organization decides to redesign its information system using only the components that are already available to it. In the language of systems theory, the resulting system would be described as a(n)

    A. ensemble   B. creod   C. kluge   D. cyborg

15. What is the term for an integrated circuit made by printing thousands or millions of transistors on a small silicon chip?

    A. Cache
    C. Control unit
    B. Semiconductor
    D. Microprocessor

16. Computer programming includes a logic pattern that allows for the repetition of certain actions while a specified condition occurs or until a certain conditions exists. This pattern is known as the

    A. object linkage
    C. key field
    B. selection construct
    D. iteration construct

17. Which of the following is the standard or reference model for allowing e-mail systems operating on different hardware to communicate?

    A. X.400   B. X.25   C. X.12   D. FDDI

18. Which of the following terms is used to denote circular tracks on the same vertical line within a disk pack?

    A. Track   B. Spindle   C. Sector   D. Cylinder

19. A system that is capable of listing the descriptions of each of a certain set of alternatives is described as

    A. generative
    B. contingency–based
    C. smart
    D. stochastic

20. Which of the following is an operating cost associated with an information system?

    A. Database establishment
    B. Facilities
    C. Personnel training
    D. Hardware acquisition

21. As a collaboration tool, the World Wide Web involves

    A. data that undergoes frequent updating
    B. documents predominantly authored by a single user
    C. applications with data at multiple sites
    D. applications with high security requirements

22. A mathematical formula used to translate a record's key field directly into its storage location is known as a(n) _____ algorithm.

    A. synchronous
    B. genetic
    C. asynchronous
    D. transform

23. Which of the following is a common DISADVANTAGE associated with outsourcing the systems development process?

    A. Loss of control over system function
    B. Increased costs
    C. Generally slow progress
    D. Increased paperwork requirements

24. Which of the following is a network topology in which all computers and other devices are connected to a central host computer?

    A. LAN   B. Star   C. Ring   D. Bus

25. In terms of information systems, *processing* means the

    A. assignment of data to certain categories for later use
    B. calculation or computation of data to arrive at a solution or conclusion
    C. conversion, manipulation, and analysis of raw input into a meaningful form
    D. collection or capture of raw data for use in an information system

KEY (CORRECT ANSWERS)

1. C
2. D
3. A
4. B
5. B

6. B
7. C
8. D
9. C
10. B

11. C
12. A
13. C
14. C
15. B

16. D
17. A
18. D
19. A
20. B

21. B
22. D
23. A
24. B
25. C

EXAMINATION SECTION
TEST 1

DIRECTIONS: Each question or incomplete statement is followed by several suggested answers or completions. Select the one the BEST answers the question or completes the statement. *PRINT THE LETTER OF THE CORRECT ANSWER IN THE SPACE AT THE RIGHT.*

1. Object-oriented programming languages include each of the following, EXCEPT 1.____

    A. Java
    B. Ada
    C. Smalltalk
    D. C++

2. _____ is a programming language that is good for processing numerical data, but does not lend itself very well to organizing large programs. 2.____

    A. Pascal
    B. Java
    C. FORTRAN
    D. COBOL

3. Which of the following is a method for insuring that a transmitted message has not been tampered with? 3.____

    A. Indexing
    B. Hashing
    C. Stringing
    D. Spoofing

4. Many expert systems use _____ programming, which is characterized by programs that are self-learning. 4.____

    A. algorithmic
    B. natural-language
    C. heuristic
    D. neural

5. Data transfer rates for devices such as hard disks are typically measured in 5.____

    A. Kbps
    B. KBps
    C. Mbps
    D. MBps

6. The most powerful way of requesting information from a database is through the use of a(n) 6.____

    A. query language
    B. menu parameter(s)
    C. query by example (QBE)
    D. query string

93

7. A network of computers located within a limited geographic area usually, a single building or group of buildingsis known as a(n)   7.___

   A. Server farm
   B. LAN
   C. MAN
   D. token ring

8. Viewing video presentations on the Web sometimes requires the use of an additional software program that adds functionality to a browser. This program is called a(n)   8.___

   A. plug-in
   B. grain
   C. applet
   D. script

9. In a _____ attack, a criminal exploits limits in the TCP/IP protocol to flood a network with useless traffic and bring it to a standstill.   9.___

   A. spoofing
   B. denial-of-service
   C. wire closet
   D. logic bomb

10. What is the term used for the technique used by some Web sites to deliver one page to a search engine for indexing while serving an entirely different page to everyone else?   10.___

    A. Diddling
    B. Port scanning
    C. Spamming
    D. Cloaking

11. _____ is a method for checking data transmission errors in which bits are added to the message and then compared against a bit that says whether the sum should be odd or even.   11.___

    A. Cyclic redundancy checking
    B. Parity checking
    C. Checksum
    D. MNP

12. A storage device's most important performance attribute is measured as   12.___

    A. latency
    B. access time
    C. permanence
    D. density

13. Most contemporary personal computers contain a CPU with a register that is _____ bits wide.   13.___

    A. 8   B. 16   C. 32   D. 64

14. A Web user wants to use a search engine for a particular color or pattern. What type of search should be used?

    A. Image content
    B. Raster-pixel
    C. Keyword
    D. Picot

15. An important difference between a router and a switcher is that a router

    A. does not perform error correction
    B. operates in software
    C. often suffers from interference
    D. is selective about the type of data it handles

16. Which of the following terms differs from the others in meaning?

    A. Software interrupt
    B. Exception
    C. Burst
    D. Trap

17. Which of the following is a database, used by the Windows operating system, that contains information about installed peripherals and software?

    A. Configuration
    B. Registry
    C. Finder
    D. Directory

18. A network server typically uses its own _____ to manage the flow of network data.

    A. RAM cache
    B. database management system
    C. virtual memory
    D. operating system

19. Which of the following types of firewall techniques applies security mechanisms whenever a TCP or UDP connection is made?

    A. Packet filter
    B. Proxy server
    C. Application gateway
    D. Circuit-level gateway

20. The frequent creation, deletion, and modification of files on a computer hard drive often leads to the condition known as

    A. clustering
    B. optimization
    C. partitioning
    D. fragmentation

21. Engineers or architects often use an output device known as a _____ to create large drawings.

    A. banner
    B. LED printer
    C. plotter
    D. thermal printer

22. In most application software, utilities such as the spell checker are usually included in the _____ menu.

    A. file
    B. edit
    C. help
    D. tools

23. The primary factor driving the use of telephone networks for the provision of Internet services throughout its first two decades was

    A. collusion between ISPs and telephone companies
    B. a lack of more suitable technologies
    C. the widespread availability of hardware and protocols
    D. the existence of analog coding for data

24. CPU clock speeds are expressed in

    A. nanoseconds
    B. MHz
    C. seconds
    D. Mbps

25. If a filename includes an extension, a(n) _____ separates the extension from the rest of the filename.

    A. period
    B. backslash
    C. parentheses
    D. space

26. Database software that uncovers previously unknown relationships among data—for example, that would reveal customers with common interests—is described as _____ software.

    A. drilldown
    B. warehousing
    C. on-line analytical processing (OLAP)
    D. data mining

27. Which of the following is a technology that combines the guaranteed delivery of circuit-switched networks and the robustness and efficiency of packet-switching networks?

    A. Frame relay
    B. DWDM
    C. SONET
    D. ATM

28. Advantages of vector graphics over bitmapped graphics include
    I. easier manipulation of images
    II. smaller memory requirements
    III. greater scalability
    IV. more refined output

    A. I and II
    B. II only
    C. II and III
    D. I, II, III and IV

29. Which of the following types of translator programs works on one line of source code at a time before execution?

    A. modulator
    B. assembler
    C. compiler
    D. interpreter

30. The protocol developed by Netscape for transmitting private documents over the Internet is

    A. Secure HTTP
    B. IPsec
    C. Secure Sockets Layer (SSL)
    D. Layer 2 Tunneling Protocol (L2TP)

31. _____ specifies the format of URLs and the procedure clients and servers follow to communicate.

    A. TCP/IP
    B. FTP
    C. HTTP
    D. HTML

32. In the 1990s, significant advancements were made in each of the following portable computing technologies, EXCEPT

    A. graphics
    B. battery performance
    C. networking capabilities
    D. storage capacity

33. Each of the following is a multimedia input device, EXCEPT

    A. image scanner
    B. digital camera
    C. microphone
    D. video camcorder

34. In a _____ network, there is no file server.

    A. two-tier
    B. three-tier
    C. peer-to-peer
    D. thin client

35. When an operating system runs different parts of a program on different processors, it is performing

    A. multiprocessing
    B. multitasking
    C. multithreading
    D. task switching

36. Hard disks
    I. generally allow for a high density of bits
    II. are much faster than floppy disks
    III. can improve their performance through caching
    IV. are the most economical form of storage

    A. I and II
    B. I, II and III
    C. II, III and IV
    D. I, II, III and IV

37. To represent a single color on a computer screen, at least _____ color values must be used.

    A. 2
    B. 3
    C. 4
    D. 5

38. The increasing popularity of the Linux operating system has been due to the fact that it is
    I. available for free
    II. platform-independent
    III. more secure than other operating systems
    IV. more user-friendly than other operating systems

    A. I and II
    B. I, II and III
    C. II only
    D. I, II, III and IV

39. The total package of protocols that specifies how a specific network functions is known as the protocol

    A. suite
    B. train
    C. stack
    D. milieu

40. Another term for the autonumber field in a database management system is _____ field.

    A. calculated
    B. key
    C. counter
    D. computational

41. Operating systems can be used to
    I. communicate with a printer
    II. format disks
    III. control the mouse cursor
    IV. save files

    A. I and II
    B. II and III
    C. II, III and IV
    D. I, II, III and IV

42. XML is a development in networking technology whose most significant contribution is in the area of

    A. functionality
    B. scalability
    C. economy
    D. interoperability

43. The most significant difference between computer viruses and Trojan horses is that

    A. Trojan horses are not destructive
    B. Trojan horses do not replicate themselves
    C. most firewalls are not built to withstand Trojan horses
    D. viruses are not disguised as useful programs

44. Slide presentation applications such as PowerPoint allow users to resize a frame within a slide by means of dragging

    A. text
    B. borders
    C. handles
    D. flaps

45. Each of the following serve to translate object code into machine language, EXCEPT

    A. binders
    B. linkers
    C. assemblers
    D. compilers

46. The most important difference between the Macintosh operating system and MS-DOS is the   46.___

    A. memory requirements
    B. functionality of drivers
    C. interface
    D. multitasking capabilities

47. Which of the following is a looser, more basic way of organizing data in order to support management decision-making?   47.___

    A. Data mart
    B. Data mine
    C. Data vault
    D. Data warehouse

48. What is the term for the amount of data that can be transmitted over a network during a fixed period of time?   48.___

    A. Bandwidth
    B. Frequency
    C. Packet volume
    D. Amplitude

49. The OSI (Open System Interconnection) model defines a networking framework for implementing protocols in seven layers. The first layer of the OSI model consists of   49.___

    A. the network
    B. transport
    C. applications
    D. hardware/physical components

50. Many paint and draw programs organize complex drawings by means of tools known as   50.___

    A. vectors
    B. sectors
    C. layers
    D. models

KEY (CORRECT ANSWERS)

1. B	11. B	21. C	31. C	41. D
2. C	12. B	22. D	32. B	42. D
3. B	13. C	23. C	33. A	43. B
4. C	14. A	24. B	34. C	44. C
5. D	15. B	25. A	35. A	45. D
6. A	16. C	26. D	36. B	46. C
7. B	17. B	27. D	37. B	47. D
8. A	18. D	28. C	38. A	48. A
9. B	19. D	29. D	39. A	49. D
10. D	20. D	30. C	40. C	50. C

TEST 2

DIRECTIONS: Each question or incomplete statement is followed by several suggested answers or completions. Select the one the BEST answers the question or completes the statement. *PRINT THE LETTER OF THE CORRECT ANSWER IN THE SPACE AT THE RIGHT.*

1. The "physical layer" of a network would include each of the following, EXCEPT

    A. RAM
    B. Error correction
    C. Virtual memory
    D. Data organization on disk

2. Servers

    A. are not designed to be used directly by the user
    B. function solely to manage network traffic
    C. often perform tasks other than their server tasks
    D. are not "computers" in the strictest sense of the word

3. Advantages of using RISC CPUs in personal computers include
    I. fewer transistors required
    II. rapid execution of instructions
    III. smaller burden placed on software

    A. I only
    B. I and II
    C. II and III
    D. I, II and III

4. Which of the following is NOT an example of middleware?

    A. Object request broker (ORB)
    B. Web server
    C. TP monitor
    D. Database access system

5. The main disadvantage to the bus network topology is its

    A. centralized point of failure
    B. high data error frequency
    C. tendency to bottleneck
    D. extensive cabling

6. Java, C++, and Perl are examples of

    A. query languages
    B. program languages
    C. markup languages
    D. application programs

7. The most significant obstacle organizations face when they try to implement ERP software is   7.____

   A. training personnel
   B. data migration
   C. reshaping business practices to conform to the system
   D. managing the up-front hardware investment

8. A storage disk's concentric circles of information, or tracks, are divided into subsections known as   8.____

   A. arcs   B. blocks   C. sectors   D. radii

9. In the client-server architecture, an ORB is sometimes necessary to   9.____

   A. provide error-checking between client and server
   B. translate the languages and protocols of distributed elements
   C. patrol the firewalls surrounding network servers
   D. help the client locate a file on a particular server

10. An office worker is proofreading a speech transcribed by a colleague. The previous worker has repeatedly and consistently misspelled the word "fiscal" as "physical." In a word processing application, the tool for automatically changing each of the misspellings is the   10.____

    A. undo command
    B. find and replace
    C. cut and paste
    D. spelling and grammar checker

11. The programs that enable a computer and its peripheral devices to function smoothly are known collectively as the   11.____

    A. operating system
    B. BIOS
    C. system software
    D. driver set

12. The act of registering a popular Internet address—usually a company name—with the intent of selling it to its rightful owner is known as   12.____

    A. spoofing
    B. steganography
    C. warchalking
    D. cybersquatting

13. A relational database management system (RDBMS) is BEST described as a database that   13.____

    A. groups related fields together in a single table
    B. organized around groups of records that have a common field value
    C. stores data in a set of associated tables
    D. helps to analyze large clusters of records

14. In object-oriented programming, a class of objects sometimes uses portions of another class in order to extend its functionality. This is a process known as

    A. inheritance
    B. annexation
    C. overlay
    D. torque

15. In digital communications, the assurance that a transferred message has been sent and received by the parties claiming to have sent and received the message is known as

    A. nonrepudiation
    B. private key encryption
    C. packet sniffing
    D. certification

16. In the hexadecimal coding system, the sequence 01001000 would represent

    A. ABC
    B. 2AC
    C. 48
    D. 136

17. The most important impact of legacy applications on software developers is a(n)

    A. large amount of time spent rewriting old code
    B. complication of bundled sales
    C. necessity for sticking with an older programming language
    D. limit placed on the functionality of new software

18. Copyrighted software that is delivered/downloaded free of charge, but requires a registration free for those who decide to keep it and use it, is known as

    A. abandonware
    B. freeware
    C. public-domain software
    D. shareware

19. _____ is a programming language that embodies powerful object-oriented features, but is complex and difficult to learn.

    A. C++
    B. Java
    C. Pascal
    D. COBOL

20. A router detects network congestion in each of the following ways, EXCEPT

    A. average queue lengths
    B. choke packet totals
    C. percentage of buffers in use
    D. line utilization

21. A Web site or service that offers a broad array of resources and services, such as e-mail, forums, search engines, and on-line shopping mallsis often referred to as a(n)   21._____

    A. site map
    B. browser
    C. host
    D. portal

22. In most Web page design software,   22._____
    I. a WYSIWYG interface is used
    II. the user is required to answer all given questions before results can be viewed
    III. the software produces HTML code
    IV. hotspots are created

    A. I and III
    B. I, III and IV
    C. II, III and IV
    D. I, II, III and IV

23. The primary difference between XML and HTML is that XML   23._____

    A. is tied to a particular applications and hardware types
    B. specifies what each data tag means
    C. contains built-in security features
    D. uses tags only to delimit items of data, and leaves interpretation up to the application that created a file

24. In draw programs, each line in a drawing is defined as a   24._____

    A. voxel
    B. bitmap
    C. pixel
    D. vector

25. "Distributions" of the Linux operating system include each of the following, EXCEPT   25._____

    A. Corel
    B. Solaris
    C. Red Hat
    D. Debian

26. Depending on the operating system, filenames may   26._____
    I. include extensions that indicate the type of file
    II. be limited in length
    III. not be permitted to use certain characters
    IV. make use of "wildcard" characters for selecting multiple files with a single selection

    A. I only
    B. I, II and III
    C. II and III
    D. I, II, III and IV

27. The "fax revolution" came about by the gradual blending of telecommunications, optical scanning, and printing technologies into a single device. This is an example of the phenomenon known as

    A. synergy
    B. coincidence
    C. asymmetry
    D. convergence

28. The security protocol most widely deployed over virtual private networks is

    A. IPsec
    B. Layer 2 tunneling protocol (L2TP)
    C. Point-to-point tunneling protocol (PPTP)
    D. Secure sockets layer (SSL)

29. The SVGA display standard supports a resolution of

    A. 640 x 480
    B. 720 x 400
    C. 800 x 600
    D. 1024 x 768

30. The expansion problems of the bus network topology are most easily solved by introducing a hub and forming a _____ topology.

    A. star
    B. line
    C. ring
    D. tree

31. When an operating system runs different parts of a program on the same processor at different times, it is performing

    A. multithreading
    B. time-sharing
    C. task switching
    D. multiprocessing

32. For long distance links, the most suitable wireless technology is

    A. radio frequencies
    B. infrared
    C. microwaves
    D. optics

33. In packet-switching networks, packets contain each of the following, EXCEPT their

    A. route through the network
    B. address of origin
    C. destination address
    D. data

34. The unit of information that precedes a data object in packet transmission, and which contains transparent information about the file or transmission, is the

   A. payload   B. comptroller   C. hash   D. header

35. What is the general term for a message given to a Web browser by a Web server?

   A. Trojan horse
   B. Cookie
   C. Token
   D. Spyware

36. In the URL *http://www.technophobia.com/index.html*, the domain name is

   A. .com
   B. technophobia.com
   C. http://www.technophobia.com
   D. technophobia

37. The purpose of a driver is to

   A. keep the CPU running at a minimum clock speed
   B. keep the bus free of interference
   C. enable the operating system to communicate with a device
   D. manage memory

38. Data on the Internet can often be manipulated dishonestly to further the agenda of the people using the data. Such methods of data manipulation include
   I. standard deviation
   II. false relevance
   III. skewed sample
   IV. deduction

   A. I and II
   B. II and III
   C. II, III and IV
   D. I, II, III and IV

39. Any circuit board in a computer that is attached directly to another board is known as a(n)

   A. controller board
   B. expansion board
   C. adapter
   D. daughtercard

40. Which of the following types of viruses propagates by means of an infected program and installs itself on the first sector of the hard disk?

   A. Trojan horse
   B. Worm
   C. MBR virus
   D. Macro virus

41. Currently, the greatest advances in the field of artificial intelligence have occurred in the field of

    A. games playing
    B. neural networks
    C. robotics
    D. expert systems

42. Most laser printers require about _____ MB of RAM to print a full-page graphic at 300 dpi.

    A. 1
    B. 2
    C. 3
    D. 5

43. In a database application, a _____ check validation would ensure that a worker's benefit eligibility status was entered into a field, rather than his/her salary or other information.

    A. consistency
    B. format
    C. range
    D. sequence

44. Heuristic programs

    A. are based on mathematically provable procedures
    B. don't usually improve over time
    C. don't always reach the very best result, but usually produce a good result
    D. are most widely used in scientific modeling

45. Which of the following types of computer programs are most susceptible to virus attacks?

    A. Operating systems
    B. Database applications
    C. Compilers
    D. Web design applications

46. The main problem with having a "fragmented" hard disk is that

    A. retrieving data can be much slower
    B. the magnetic charge on the disk is weakened
    C. the disk cache is inhibited by interference
    D. it becomes impossible to move data from one location to another

47. The OSI (Open System Interconnection) model defines a networking framework for implementing protocols in seven layers. The _____ layer, or layer 5, establishes, manages and terminates connections between applications.

    A. Transport
    B. Data link
    C. Session
    D. Network

48. Management information systems are typically written in   48._____

    A. FORTRAN
    B. C
    C. COBOL
    D. BASIC

49. Because each command is executed independently, without any knowledge of the commands that came before it, HTTP is described as a(n) _____ protocol.   49._____

    A. shallow
    B. isolate
    C. stateless
    D. marooned

50. Advantages of fiber optic communications over traditional metal lines include   50._____
    I. greater bandwidth
    II. more lightweight
    III. less interference
    IV. sturdier and more durable

    A. I only
    B. I, II, III
    C. II and III
    D. I, II, III and IV

KEY (CORRECT ANSWERS)

1. C	11. C	21. D	31. B	41. A
2. A	12. D	22. B	32. C	42. A
3. B	13. C	23. D	33. A	43. B
4. B	14. A	24. D	34. D	44. C
5. A	15. A	25. B	35. B	45. A
6. B	16. C	26. D	36. B	46. A
7. C	17. D	27. D	37. C	47. C
8. C	18. D	28. A	38. B	48. C
9. B	19. A	29. C	39. D	49. C
10. B	20. B	30. A	40. C	50. B

EXAMINATION SECTION
TEST 1

DIRECTIONS: Each question or incomplete statement is followed by several suggested answers or completions. Select the one that BEST answers the question or completes the statement. *PRINT THE LETTER OF THE CORRECT ANSWER IN THE SPACE AT THE RIGHT.*

1. Which of the following words in a pseudocode statement can be replaced by the word *read*?
    A. Get   B. Print   C. Set   D. Store

2. Units of input and output in pseudocode are known as
    A. lines   B. items   C. strings   D. records

3. The statement required to print the value of number of students followed by the label PEOPLE would be written:
    A. Set value to PEOPLE
    B. Print *number of students* and PEOPLE
    C. Read *number of students* and PEOPLE
    D. Write *number of students* and PEOPLE

4. What command word is used to save contents of another storage location or a constant in a storage location?
    A. Store   B. Set   C. Get   D. Put

5. The symbol used for multiplication in pseudocode is
    A. –   B. /   C. *   D. x

6. A statement constructed to give the first number in a data set the same value as the second number would be expressed as _____ first number _____ second number.
    A. read; as   B. set; to
    C. declare; as   D. —; =

7. The function of a literal is to
    A. read stored values
    B. identify or describe output
    C. write results
    D. store input values

8. What is the term for a grouping of items that have a similar characteristic or common identifying property?
    A. Set   B. Array
    C. String   D. Assortment

9. When calculations are written in algebraic expression, the name of the storage location in which the result would be *save* is expressed as
    A. zero   B. =   C. x   D. y

111

10. If a value of 10 is stored in memory at X, the output that the statement *Print 'X'* would produce is

    A. 10
    B. 'X'
    C. X
    D. X = 10

11. Which of the following steps in using a subprogram would occur FIRST?

    A. Subprogram executed
    B. Subprogram invoked
    C. Program continues execution
    D. Results passed through program

12. A declaration for the data item *inventory item stock number* would be written: Declare

    A. stock number, numeric inventory item
    B. numeric inventory item stock number
    C. inventory item stock number
    D. character inventory item stock number

13. Of the following, a(n) _____ is NOT always an element of the *loop while* construct.

    A. *end loop* statement
    B. counter
    C. group of one or more statements forming the loop body
    D. means of making the *loop while* condition false

14. Information is placed into a storage location by means of a(n) _____ statement.

    A. call
    B. assignment
    C. return
    D. address

15. A programmer wants to place a zero into a memory location that is to contain a counter. Each of the following is a possible statement EXCEPT:

    A. Set counter to zero
    B. Initialize zero in counter
    C. Set COUNT to zero
    D. Store zero in counter

16. What is the term used for the items of information necessary for a program or subprogram to perform its task?

    A. Records
    B. Functions
    C. Parameters
    D. Constructs

17. Which of the following items of input would be needed in order to construct a module that finds the sum of two arrays, A and B?
    The

    A. number of elements in A and B
    B. loop for J = 1 to the number of elements in A and B
    C. two numbers, J and K
    D. sum of the two arrays

18. A statement constructed to initialize a total cost at zero would be written:

    A. Set total cost to zero
    B. Set zero to total cost
    C. Total cost =0
    D. Read total cost as zero

19. In order to provide a means of executing a named block of statements, the _____ is used.

    A. call statement
    B. selection parameter
    C. return statement
    D. do module

20. Each element in an array is identified by a number called a _____, which designates position in the array.

    A. marker
    B. literal
    C. string
    D. subscript

21. A value of 8 is stored in memory at X.
    The following statement would produce the output X = 8.

    A. Print X = 8
    B. Read X as 8
    C. Print 'X =' and X
    D. Print 'X = 8'

22. The symbol for division in pseudocode is

    A. —
    B. ∫
    C. ÷
    D. /

23. A data item is denoted as non-numeric by means of a(n)

    A. record
    B. string
    C. address
    D. name

24. A statement constructed to set the value of an employee count to zero would be written:

    A. Get zero employee count
    B. Read zero for employee count
    C. Set employee count to zero
    D. Put employee count at zero

25. Which of the following key words is NOT used for the purpose of selection in pseudocode?

    A. Else
    B. Then
    C. While
    D. If

KEY (CORRECT ANSWERS)

1.	A	11.	B
2.	D	12.	D
3.	D	13.	B
4.	B	14.	B
5.	C	15.	B
6.	B	16.	C
7.	B	17.	A
8.	B	18.	A
9.	C	19.	D
10.	C	20.	D

21. C
22. D
23. B
24. C
25. C

TEST 2

DIRECTIONS: Each question or incomplete statement is followed by several suggested answers or completions. Select the one that BEST answers the question or completes the statement. *PRINT THE LETTER OF THE CORRECT ANSWER IN THE SPACE AT THE RIGHT.*

1. To perform loop operation, each of the following must be done to the counter EXCEPT   1._____

    A. division
    B. initialization
    C. testing
    D. incrementation

2. A subprogram that finds the largest element in an array can be constructed as a   2._____

    A. loop
    B. function
    C. loop with counter
    D. do module

3. *Read employee's name, hourly pay rate, number of hours worked, and gross pay.*   3._____
   In the above statement, the optional word is

    A. rate   B. and   C. number   D. read

4. *Find degrees Fahrenheit by multiplying degrees centigrade by nine-fifths and adding 32 to the result.*   4._____
   To compute and save the result for the above, the required statement using algebraic form would be written:

    A. F = ((9*C)/5) + 32
    B. F = (9/5)xC) + 32
    C. Set F to ((9.C/5) + 32
    D. F = 9/5C + 32

5. Output in pseudocode is indicated by each of the following key words EXCEPT   5._____

    A. print   B. get   C. write   D. put

6. The _____ statement is placed at the bottom of a selection group.   6._____

    A. call   B. return   C. do   D. end if

7. A statement constructed to save 100 in number of people would be written: 7._____

    A. Read 100 for number of people
    B. Store 100 for number of people
    C. Set 100 for number of people
    D. Set number of people to 100

8. In pseudocode, the *loop with counter* construct is specified by the key words   8._____

    A. loop while
    B. end loop
    C. loop for
    D. end if

9. A programmer wishes to construct a nested selection to handle the following case: Add 1 to senior resident counter when town residence is Oakville and person's age is greater than 64.   9._____
   In the best logical construction, the statement would begin:

115

A. Others counter = others counter + 1
B. If town of residence is Oakville
C. If age is greater than 64
D. Senior residence counter = senior resident counter + 1

10. Which of the following terms is NOT used to indicate the meaning of output in pseudocode?

    A. Character string
    B. Label
    C. Record
    D. Literal

11. What kind of statement is used to revert control to a calling program?

    A. Call
    B. End loop
    C. Return
    D. Reassignment

12. The statement required to save the literal SUSPENDED in student status would be written:

    A. Write student status as SUSPENDED
    B. Get SUSPENDED to student status
    C. Set student status to 'SUSPENDED'
    D. Read student status as 'SUSPENDED'

13. Which of the following words in a pseudocode statement can be replaced by the word *print*?

    A. Get   B. Print   C. Set   D. Store

14. In pseudocode, the = symbol indicates

    A. division
    B. an equality of values
    C. a read command
    D. a storage assignment for information

15. Which of the following steps in using a subprogram would occur LAST?

    A. Subprogram executed
    B. Subprogram invoked
    C. Program continues execution
    D. Results passed through program

16. If a value of 10 is stored in memory at X, the statement *Print X* will produce the output

    A. 10   B. 'X'   C. X   D. X = 10

17. Which of the following is NOT an example of a non-numeric data item?

    A. Telephone number
    B. ZIP code
    C. Student identification number
    D. Temperature

18. For moving the contents of one storage location to another location in algebraic expression, a statement of the form _____ should be used. 18._____

    A. x = y
    B. Move x to y
    C. x/y
    D. Set x to y

19. A declaration for the data item *number of employees* would be written: Declare 19._____

    A. employees, number of
    B. numeric number of employees
    C. number of employees
    D. character number of employees

20. In a *loop while* construct, the loop will be terminated upon the introduction of a(n) 20._____

    A. false condition
    B. return statement
    C. subprogram
    D. *end if* statement

21. The statement required to print the message GROSS PAY IS $ followed by the value of gross pay would be written: 21._____

    A. Get gross pay and GROSS PAY IS $
    B. Read 'GROSS PAY IS $' and gross pay
    C. Write 'GROSS PAY IS $' and gross pay
    D. Print 'GROSS PAY IS $' and gross pay

22. In pseudocode, the value x^2 would be written 22._____

    A. X-2
    B. X**2
    C. X//2
    D. X*2

23. A statement using algebraic form to compute and save the result for *Add one to number of days* would be written: 23._____

    A. Number of days + 1
    B. Number of days = number of days + 1
    C. Set number of days to number of days + 1
    D. Set number of days + 1

24. What type of statement is used to invoke a subprogram? 24._____

    A. Do
    B. Call
    C. Assignment
    D. Return

25. A programmer wants to construct a statement that instructs the computer to print the message *There is no sales tax* if the tax code is zero and *The sales tax is 4%* otherwise. In the statement, what would follow the key word *else*? 25._____

    A. Write 'There is no sales tax'
    B. Get tax code
    C. Write 'The sales tax is 4%'
    D. Set tax code to zero

KEY (CORRECT ANSWERS)

1. A
2. B
3. B
4. A
5. B

6. D
7. D
8. C
9. C
10. C

11. C
12. C
13. B
14. D
15. C

16. A
17. D
18. A
19. B
20. A

21. C
22. B
23. B
24. B
25. C

PREPARING WRITTEN MATERIAL

PARAGRAPH REARRANGEMENT
COMMENTARY

The sentences that follow are in scrambled order. You are to rearrange them in proper order and indicate the letter choice containing the correct answer at the space at the right.

Each group of sentences in this section is actually a paragraph presented in scrambled order. Each sentence in the group has a place in that paragraph; no sentence is to be left out. You are to read each group of sentences and decide upon the best order in which to put the sentences so as to form a well-organized paragraph.

The questions in this section measure the ability to solve a problem when all the facts relevant to its solution are not given.

More specifically, certain positions of responsibility and authority require the employee to discover connection between events sometimes, apparently, unrelated. In order to do this, the employee will find it necessary to correctly infer that unspecified events have probably occurred or are likely to occur. This ability becomes especially important when action must be taken on incomplete information.

Accordingly, these questions require competitors to choose among several suggested alternatives, each of which presents a different sequential arrangement of the events. Competitors must choose the MOST logical of the suggested sequences.

In order to do so, they may be required to draw on general knowledge to infer missing concepts or events that are essential to sequencing the given events. Competitors should be careful to infer only what is essential to the sequence. The plausibility of the wrong alternatives will always require the inclusion of unlikely events or of additional chains of events which are NOT essential to sequencing the given events.

It's very important to remember that you are looking for the best of the four possible choices, and that the best choice of all may not even be one of the answers you're given to choose from.

There is no one right way to solve these problems. Many people have found it helpful to first write out the order of the sentences, as they would have arranged them, on their scrap paper before looking at the possible answers. If their optimum answer is there, this can save them some time. If it isn't, this method can still give insight into solving the problem. Others find it most helpful to just go through each of the possible choices, contrasting each as they go along. You should use whatever method feels comfortable and works for you.

While most of these types of questions are not that difficult, we've added a higher percentage of the difficult type, just to give you more practice. Usually there are only one or two questions on this section that contain such subtle distinctions that you're unable to answer confidently. And you then may find yourself stuck deciding between two possible choices, neither of which you're sure about.

EXAMINATION SECTION

TEST 1

DIRECTIONS: The following groups of sentences need to be arranged in an order that makes sense. Select the letter preceding the sequence that represents the BEST sentence order. *PRINT THE LETTER OF THE CORRECT ANSWER IN THE SPACE AT THE RIGHT.*

1.
   I. The keyboard was purposely designed to be a little awkward to slow typists down.
   II. The arrangement of letters on the keyboard of a typewriter was not designed for the convenience of the typist.
   III. Fortunately, no one is suggesting that a new keyboard be designed right away.
   IV. If one were, we would have to learn to type all over again.
   V. The reason was that the early machines were slower than the typists and would jam easily.
   The CORRECT answer is:
   A. I, III, IV, II, V
   B. II, V, I, IV, III
   C. V, I, II, III, IV
   D. II, I, V, III, IV

2.
   I. The majority of the new service jobs are part-time or low-paying.
   II. According to the U.S. Bureau of Labor Statistics, jobs in the service sector constitute 72% of all jobs in this country.
   III. If more and more workers receive less and less money, who will buy the goods and services needed to keep the economy going?
   IV. The service sector is by far the fastest growing part of the United States economy.
   V. Some economists look upon this trend with great concern.
   The CORRECT answer is:
   A. II, IV, I, V, III
   B. II, III, IV, I, V
   C. V, IV, II, III, I
   D. III, I, II, IV, V

3.
   I. They can also affect one's endurance.
   II. This can stabilize blood sugar levels, and ensure that the brain is receiving a steady, constant, supply of glucose, so that one is *hitting on all cylinders* while taking the test.
   III. By food, we mean real food, not junk food or unhealthy snacks.
   IV. For this reason, it is important not to skip a meal, and to bring food with you to the exam.
   V. One's blood sugar levels can affect how clearly one is able to think and concentrate during an exam.
   The CORRECT answer is:
   A. V, IV, II, III, I
   B. V, II, I, IV, III
   C. V, I, IV, III, II
   D. V, IV, I, III, II

4. I. Those who are the embodiment of desire are absorbed in material quests, and those who are the embodiment of feeling are warriors who value power more than possession.
    II. These qualities are in everyone, but in different degrees.
    III. But those who value understanding yearn not for goods or victory, but for knowledge.
    IV. According to Plato, human behavior flows from three main sources: desire, emotion, and knowledge.
    V. In the perfect state, the industrial forces would produce but not rule, the military would protect but not rule, and the forces of knowledge, the philosopher kings, would reign.
    The CORRECT answer is:
    A. IV, V, I, II, III
    B. V, I, II, III, IV
    C. IV, III, II, I, V
    D. IV, II, I, III, V

5. I. Of the more than 26,000 tons of garbage produced daily in New York City, 12,000 tons arrive daily at Fresh Kills.
    II. In a month, enough garbage accumulates there to fill the Empire State Building.
    III. In 1937, the Supreme Court halted the practice of dumping the trash of New York City into the sea.
    IV. Although the garbage is compacted, in a few years the mounds of garbage at Fresh Kills will be the highest points south of Maine's Mount Desert Island on the Eastern Seaboard.
    V. Instead, tugboats now pull barges of much of the trash to Staten Island and the largest landfill in the world, Fresh Kills.
    The CORRECT answer is:
    A. III, V, IV, I, II
    B. III, V, II, IV, I
    C. III, V, I, II, IV
    D. III, II, V, IV, I

6. I. Communists rank equality very high, but freedom very low.
    II. Unlike communists, conservatives place a high value on freedom and a very low value on equality.
    III. A recent study demonstrated that one way to classify people's political beliefs is to look at the importance placed on two words: freedom and equality.
    IV. Thus, by demonstrating how members of these groups feel about the two words, the study has proved to be useful for political analysts in several European countries.
    V. According to the study, socialists and liberals rank both freedom and equality very high, while fascists rate both very low.
    The CORRECT answer is:
    A. III, V, I, II, IV
    B. V, IV, III, I, II
    C. III, V, IV, II, I
    D. III, I, II, IV, V

7. I. "Can there be anything more amazing than this?"
    II. If the riddle is successfully answered, his dead brothers will be brought back to life.
    III. "Even though man sees those around him dying every day," says Dharmaraj, "he still believes and acts as if he were immortal."
    IV. "What is the cause of ceaseless wonder?" asks the Lord of the Lake.
    V. In the ancient epic, The Mahabharata, a riddle is asked of one of the Pandava brothers.
    The CORRECT answer is:
    A. V, II, I, IV, III B. V, IV, III, I, II
    C. V, II, IV, III, I D. V, II, IV, I, III

8. I. On the contrary, the two main theories—the cooperative (neoclassical) theory and the radical (labor theory)—clearly rest on very different assumptions, which have very different ethical overtones.
    II. The distribution of income is the primary factor in determining the relative levels of material well-being that different groups or individuals attain.
    III. Of all issues in economics, the distribution of income is one of the most controversial.
    IV. The neoclassical theory tends to support the existing income distribution (or minor changes), while the labor theory ends to support substantial changes in the way income is distributed.
    V. The intensity of the controversy reflects the fact that different economic theories are not purely neutral, *detached* theories with no ethical or moral implications.
    The CORRECT answer is:
    A. II, I, V, IV, III B. III, II, V, I, IV
    C. III, V, II, I, IV D. III, V, IV, I, II

9. I. The pool acts as a broker and ensures that the cheapest power gets used first.
    II. Every six seconds, the pool's computer monitors all of the generating stations in the state and decides which to ask for more power and which to cut back.
    III. The buying and selling of electrical power is handled by the New York Power Pool in Guilderland, New York.
    IV. This is to the advantage of both the buying and selling utilities.
    V. The pool began operation in 1970, and consists of the state's eight electric utilities.
    The CORRECT answer is:
    A. V, I, II, III, IV B. IV, II, I, III, V
    C. III, V, I, IV, II D. V, III, IV, II, I

10. I. Modern English is much simpler grammatically than Old English.
    II. Finnish grammar is very complicated; there are some fifteen cases, for example.
    III. Chinese, a very old language, may seem to be the exception, but it is the great number of characters/words that must be mastered that makes it so difficult to learn, not its grammar.
    IV. The newest literary language—that is, written as well as spoken—is Finish, whose literary roots go back only to about the middle of the nineteenth century.
    V. Contrary to popular belief, the longer a language is been in use the simpler its grammar—not the reverse.

    The CORRECT answer is:
    A. IV, I, II, III, V
    B. V, I, IV, II, III
    C. I, II, IV, III, V
    D. IV, II, III, I, V

10.____

KEY (CORRECT ANSWERS)

1. D   6. A
2. A   7. C
3. C   8. B
4. D   9. C
5. C   10. B

TEST 2

DIRECTIONS: This type of question tests your ability to recognize accurate paraphrasing, well-constructed paragraphs, and appropriate style and tone. It is important that the answer you select contains only the facts or concepts given in the original sentences. It is also important that you be aware of incomplete sentences, inappropriate transitions, unsupported opinions, incorrect usage, and illogical sentence order. Paragraphs that do not include all the necessary facts and concepts, that distort them, or that add new ones are not considered correct.

The format for this section may vary. Sometimes, long paragraphs are given, and emphasis is placed on style and organization. Our first five questions are of this type. Other times, the paragraphs are shorter, and there is less emphasis on style and more emphasis on accurate representation of information. Our second group of five questions are of this nature.

For each of Questions 1 through 10, select the paragraph that BEST expresses the ideas contained in the sentences above it. *PRINT THE LETTER OF THE CORRECT ANSWER IN THE SPACE AT THE RIGHT.*

1. I. Listening skills are very important for managers.
    II. Listening skills are not usually emphasized.
    III. Whenever managers are depicted in books, manuals or the media, they are always talking, never listening.
    IV. We'd like you to read the enclosed handout on listening skills and to try to consciously apply them this week.
    V. We guarantee they will improve the quality of your interactions.

    A. Unfortunately, listening skills are not usually emphasized for managers. Managers are always depicted as talking, never listening. We'd like you to read the enclosed handout on listening skills. Please try to apply these principles this week. If you do, we guarantee they will improve the quality of your interactions.
    B. The enclosed handout on listening skills will be important improving the quality of your interactions. We guarantee it. All you have to do is take sometime this week to read and to consciously try to apply the principles. Listening skills are very important for manages, but they are not usually emphasized. Whenever managers are depicted in books, manuals or the media, they are always talking, never listening.
    C. Listening well is one of the most important skills a manager can have, yet it's not usually given much attention. Think about any representation of managers in books, manuals, or in the media that you may have seen. They're always talking, never listening. We'd like you to read the enclosed handout on listening skills and consciously try to apply them the rest of the week. We guarantee you will see a difference in the quality of your interactions.

1.____

D. Effective listening, one very important tool in the effective manager's arsenal, is usually not emphasized enough. The usual depiction of managers in books, manuals or the media is one in which they are always talking, never listening. We'd like you to read the enclosed handout and consciously try to apply the information contained therein throughout the rest of the week. We feel sure that you will see a marked difference in the quality of your interactions.

2.
I. Chekhov wrote three dramatic masterpieces which share certain themes and formats: <u>Uncle Vanya</u>, <u>The Cherry Orchard</u>, and <u>The Three Sisters</u>.
II. They are primarily concerned with the passage of time and how this erodes human aspirations.
III. The plays are haunted by the ghosts of the wasted life.
IV. The characters are concerned with life's lesser problems; however, such as the inability to make decisions, loyalty to the wrong cause, and the inability to be clear.
V. This results in sweet, almost aching, type of a sadness referred to as Chekhovian.

2._____

A. Chekhov wrote three dramatic masterpieces: <u>Uncle Vanya</u>, <u>The Cherry Orchard</u>, and <u>The Three Sisters</u>. These masterpieces share certain themes and formats: the passage of time, how time erodes human aspirations, and the ghosts of wasted life. Each masterpiece is characterized by a sweet, almost aching, type of sadness that has become known as Chekhovian. The sweetness of this sadness hinges on the fact that it is not the great tragedies of life which are destroying these characters, but their minor flaws: indecisiveness, misplaced loyalty, unclarity.

B. <u>The Cherry Orchard</u>, <u>Uncle Vanya</u>, and <u>The Three Sisters</u> are three dramatic masterpieces written by Chekhov that use similar formats to explore a common theme. Each is primarily concerned with the way that passing time wears down human aspirations, and each is haunted by the ghosts of the wasted life. The characters are shown struggling futilely with the lesser problems of life: indecisiveness, loyalty to the wrong cause, and the inability to be clear. These struggles create a mood of sweet, almost aching, sadness that has become known as Chekhovian.

C. Chekhov's dramatic masterpieces are, along with <u>The Cherry Orchard</u>, <u>Uncle Vanya</u>, and <u>The Three Sisters</u>. These plays share certain thematic and formal similarities. They are concerned most of all with the passage of time and the way in which time erodes human aspirations. Each play is haunted by the specter of the wasted life. Chekhov's characters are caught, however, by life's lesser snares: indecisiveness, loyalty to the wrong cause, and unclarity. The characteristic mood is a sweet, almost aching type of sadness that has come to be known as Chekhovian.

D. A Chekhovian mood is characterized by sweet, almost aching, sadness. The term comes from three dramatic tragedies by Chekhov which revolve around the sadness of a wasted life. The three masterpieces (<u>Uncle Vanya</u>, <u>The Three Sisters</u>, and <u>The Cherry Orchard</u>) share the same theme and format. The plays are concerned with how the passage of time erodes human aspirations. They are peopled with characters who are struggling with life's lesser problems. These are people who are indecisive, loyal to the wrong causes, or are unable to make themselves clear.

3.
  I. Movie previews have often helped producers decide which parts of movies they should take out or leave in.
  II. The first 1933 preview of King Kong was very helpful to the producers because many people ran screaming from the theater and would not return when four men first attacked by Kong were eaten by giant spiders.
  III. The 1950 premiere of Sunset Boulevard resulted in the filming of an entirely new beginning, and a delay of six months in the film's release.
  IV. In the original opening scene, William Holden was in a morgue talking with thirty-six other "corpses" about the ways some of them had died.
  V. When he began to tell them of his life with Gloria Swanson, the audience found this hilarious, instead of taking the scene seriously.

3.____

  A. Movie previews have often helped producers decide what parts of movies they should leave in or take out. For example, the first preview of King Kong in 1933 was very helpful. In one scene, four men were first attacked by Kong and then eaten by giant spiders. Many members of the audience ran screaming from the theater and would not return. The premiere of the 1950 film Sunset Boulevard was also very helpful. In the original opening scene, William Holden was in a morgue with thirty-six other "corpses," discussing the ways some of them had died. When he began to tell them of his life with Gloria Swanson, the audience found this hilarious. They were supposed to take the scene seriously. The result was a delay of six months in the release of the film while a new beginning was added.
  B. Movie previews have often helped producers decide whether they should change various parts of a movie. After the 1933 preview of King Kong, a scene in which four men who had been attacked by Kong were eaten by giant spiders was taken out as many people ran screaming from the theater and would not return. The 1950 premiere of Sunset Boulevard also led to some changes. In the original opening scene, William Holden was in a morgue talking with thirty-six other "corpses" about the ways some of them had died. When he began to tell them of his life with Gloria Swanson, the audience found this hilarious, instead of taking the scene seriously.
  C. What do Sunset Boulevard and King Kong have in common? Both show the value of using movie previews to test audience reaction. The first 1933 preview of King Kong showed that a scene showing four men being eaten by giant spiders after having been attacked by Kong was too frightening for many people. They ran screaming from the theater and couldn't be coaxed back. The 1950 premiere of Sunset Boulevard was also a scream, but not the kind the producers intended. The movie opens

with William Holden lying in a morgue discussing the ways they had died with thirty-six other "corpses." When he began to tell them of his life with Gloria Swanson, the audience couldn't take him seriously. Their laughter caused a six-month delay while the beginning was rewritten.

D. Producers very often use movie previews to decide if changes are needed. The premiere of Sunset Boulevard in 1950 led to a new beginning and a six-month delay in film release. At the beginning, William Holden and thirty-six other "corpses" discuss the ways some of them died. Rather than taking this seriously, the audience thought it was hilarious when he began to tell them of his life with Gloria Swanson. The first 1933 preview of King Kong was very helpful for its producers because one scene so terrified the audience that many of them ran screaming from the theater and would not return. In this particular scene, four men who had first been attacked by Kong were eaten by giant spiders.

4.
I. It is common for supervisors to view employees as "things" to be manipulated. 4.____
II. This approach does not motivate employees, nor does the carrot-and-stick approach because employees often recognize these behaviors and resent them.
III. Supervisors can change these behaviors by using self-inquiry and persistence.
IV. The best managers genuinely respect those they work with, are supportive and helpful, and are interested in working as a team with those they supervise.
V. They disagree with the Golden Rule that says "he or she who has the gold makes the rules."

A. Some managers act as if they think the Golden Rule means "he or she who has the gold makes the rules." They show disrespect to employees by seeing them as "things" to be manipulated. Obviously, this approach does not motivate employees any more than the carrot-and-stick approach motivates them. The employees are smart enough to spot these behaviors and resent them. On the other hand, the managers genuinely respect those they work with, are supportive and helpful, and are interested in working as a team. Self-inquiry and persistence can change even the former type of supervisor into the latter.

B. Many supervisors all into the trap of viewing employees as "things" to be manipulated, or try to motivate them by using a carrot-and-stick approach. These methods do not motivate employees, who often recognize the behaviors and resent them. Supervisors can change these behaviors, however, by using self-inquiry and persistence. The best managers are supportive and helpful, and have genuine respect for those with whom they work. They are interested in working as a team with those they supervise. To them, the Golden Rule is not "he or she who has the gold makes the rules."

C. Some supervisors see employees as "things" to be used or manipulated using a carrot-and-stick technique. These methods don't work. Employees often see through them and resent them. A supervisor who wants to change may do so. The techniques of self-inquiry and persistence can be used to turn him or her into the type of supervisor who doesn't think the Golden Rule is "he or she who has the gold makes the rules." They may become like the best managers who treat those with whom they work with respect and give them help and support. These are the manager who know how to build a team.

D. Unfortunately, many supervisors act as if their employees are objects whose movements they can position at will. This mistaken belief has the same result as another popular motivational technique—the carrot-and-stick approach. Both attitudes can lead to the same result—resentment from those employees who recognize the behaviors for what they are. Supervisors who recognize these behaviors can change through the use of persistence and the use of self-inquiry. It's important to remember that the best managers respect their employees. They readily give necessary help and support and are interested in working as a team with those they supervise. To these managers, the Golden Rule is not "he or she who has the gold makes the rules."

5.
I. The first half of the nineteenth century produced a group of pessimistic poets—Byron, De Musset, Heine, Pushkin, and Leopardi.
II. It also produced a group of pessimistic composers—Schubert, Chopin, Schumann, and even the later Beethoven.
III. Above all, in philosophy, there was the profoundly pessimistic philosopher, Schopenhauer.
IV. The Revolution was dead, the Bourbons were restored, the feudal barons were reclaiming their land, and progress everywhere was being suppressed, as the great age was over.
V. "I thank God," said Goethe, "that I am not young in so thoroughly finished a world."

5._____

A. "I thank God," said Goethe, "that I am not young in so thoroughly finished a world." The Revolution was dead, the Bourbons were restored, the feudal barons were reclaiming their land, and progress everywhere was being suppressed. The first half of the nineteenth century produced a group of pessimistic poets: Byron, De Musset, Heine, Pushkin, and Leopardi. It also produced pessimistic composers: Schubert, Chopin, Schumann. Although Beethoven came later, he fits into this group, too. Finally and above all, it also produced a profoundly pessimistic philosopher, Schopenhauer. The great age was over.

B. The first half of the nineteenth century produced a group of pessimistic poets: Byron, De Musset, Heine, Pushkin, and Leopardi. It produced a group of pessimistic composers: Schubert, Chopin, Schumann, and even the later Beethoven. Above all, it produced a profoundly pessimistic philosopher, Schopenhauer. For each of these men, the great age was over. The Revolution was dead, and the Bourbons were restored. The feudal barons were reclaiming their land, and progress everywhere was being suppressed.

C. The great age was over. The Revolution was dead—the Bourbons were restored, and the feudal barons were reclaiming their land. Progress everywhere was being suppressed. Out of this climate came a profound pessimism. Poets, like Byron, De Musset, Heine, Pushkin, and Leopardi; composers, like Schubert, Chopin, Schumann, and even the later Beethoven; and above all, a profoundly pessimistic philosopher, Schopenauer. This pessimism which arose in the first half of the nineteenth century is illustrated by these words of Goethe, "I thank God that I am not young in so thoroughly finished a world."
D. The first half of the nineteenth century produced a group of pessimistic poets, Byron, De Musset, Heine, Pushkin, and Leopardi—and a group of pessimistic composers, Schubert, Chopin, Schumann, and the later Beethoven. Above it all, it produced a profoundly pessimistic philosopher, Schopenhauer. The great age was over. The Revolution was dead, the Bourbons were restored, the feudal barons were reclaiming their land, and progress everywhere was being suppressed. "I thank God," said Goethe, "that I am not young in so thoroughly finished a world."

6. I. A new manager sometimes may feel insecure about his or her competence in the new position.
    II. The new manager may then exhibit defensive or arrogant behavior towards those one supervises, or the new manager may direct overly flattering behavior toward one's new supervisor.

    A. Sometimes, a new manager may feel insecure about his or her ability to perform well in this new position. The insecurity may lead him or her to treat others differently. He or she may display arrogant or defensive behavior towards those he or she supervises, or be overly flattering to his or her new supervisor.
    B. A new manager may sometimes feel insecure about his or her ability to perform well in the new position. He or she may then become arrogant, defensive, or overly flattering towards those he or she works with.
    C. There are times when a new manager may be insecure about how well he or she can perform in the new job. The new manager may also behave defensive or act in an arrogant way towards those he or she supervises, or overly flatter his or her boss.
    D. Sometimes a new manager may feel insecure about his or her ability to perform well in the new position. He or she may then display arrogant or defensive behavior towards those they supervise, or become overly flattering towards their supervisors.

6._____

7. I. It is possible to eliminate unwanted behavior by bringing it under stimulus control—tying the behavior to a cue, and then never, or rarely, giving the cue.
    II. One trainer successfully used this method to keep an energetic young porpoise from coming out of her tank whenever she felt like it, which was potentially dangerous.
    III. Her trainer taught her to do it for a reward, in response to a hand signal, and then rarely gave the signal.

7._____

A. Unwanted behavior can be eliminated by tying the behavior to a cue, and then never, or rarely, giving the cue. This is called stimulus control. One trainer was able to use this method to keep an energetic young porpoise from coming out of her tank by teaching her to come out for a reward in response to a hand signal, and then rarely giving the signal.
B. Stimulus control can be used to eliminate unwanted behavior. In this method, behavior is tied to a cue, and then the cue is rarely, if ever, given. One trainer was able to successfully use stimulus control to keep an energetic young porpoise from coming out of her tank whenever she felt like it—a potentially dangerous practice. She taught the porpoise to come out for a reward when she gave a hand signal, and then rarely gave the signal.
C. It is possible to eliminate behavior that is undesirable by bringing it under stimulus control by tying behavior to a signal, and then rarely giving the signal. One trainer successfully used this method to keep an energetic porpoise from coming out of her tank, a potentially dangerous situation. Her trainer taught the porpoise to do it for a reward, in response to a hand signal, and then would rarely give the signal.
D. By using stimulus control, it is possible to eliminate unwanted behavior by tying the behavior to a cue, and then rarely or never give the cue. One trainer was able to use this method to successfully stop a young porpoise from coming out of her tank whenever she felt like it. To curb this potentially dangerous practice, the porpoise was taught by the trainer to come out of the tank for a reward, in response to a hand signal, and then rarely given the signal.

8. I.   There is a great deal of concern over the safety of commercial trucks, caused by their greatly increased role in serious accidents since federal deregulation in 1981.
    II. Recently, 60 percent of trucks in New York and Connecticut and 70 percent of trucks in Maryland randomly stopped by state troopers failed safety inspections.
    III. Sixteen states in the United States require no training at all for truck drivers.

    A. Since federal deregulation in 1981, there has been a great deal of concern over the safety of commercial trucks, and their greatly increased role in serious accidents. Recently, 60 percent of trucks in New York and Connecticut, and 70 percent of trucks in Maryland failed safety inspections. Sixteen states in the United States require no training at all for truck drivers.
    B. There is a great deal of concern over the safety of commercial trucks since federal deregulation in 1981. Their role in serious accidents has greatly increased. Recently, 60 percent of trucks randomly stopped in Connecticut and New York and 70 percent in Maryland failed safety inspections conducted by state troopers. Sixteen states in the United States provide no training at all for truck drivers.
    C. Commercial trucks have a greatly increased role in serious accidents since federal deregulation in 1981. This has led to a great deal of concern.

8.____

Recently, 70 percent of trucks in Maryland and 60 percent of trucks in New York and Connecticut failed inspection of those that were randomly stopped by state troopers. Sixteen states in the United States require no training for all truck drivers.

D. Since federal deregulation in 1981, the role that commercial trucks have played in serious accidents has greatly increased, and this has led to a great deal of concern. Recently, 60 percent of trucks in New York and Connecticut, and 70 percent of trucks in Maryland randomly stopped by state troopers failed safety inspections. Sixteen states in the U.S. don't require any training for truck drivers.

9. I. No matter how much some people have, they still feel unsatisfied and want more, or want to keep what they have forever.
    II. One recent television documentary showed several people flying from New York to Paris for a one-day shopping spree to buy platinum earrings, because they were bored.
    III. In Brazil, some people were ordering coffins that cost a minimum of $45,000 and are equipping them with deluxe stereos, televisions, and other graveyard necessities.

    9.____

   A. Some people, despite having a great deal, still feel unsatisfied and want more, or think they can keep what they have forever. One recent documentary on television showed several people enroute from Paris to New York for a one day shopping spree to buy platinum earrings, because they were bored. Some people in Brazil are even ordering coffins equipped with such graveyard necessities as deluxe stereos and televisions. The price of the coffins start at $45,000.
   B. No matter how much some people have, they may feel unsatisfied. This leads them to want more, or to want to keep what they have forever. Recently, a television documentary depicting several people flying from New York to Paris for a one day shopping spree to buy platinum earrings. They were bored. Some people in Brazil are ordering coffins that cost at least $45,000 and come equipped with deluxe televisions, stereos and other necessary graveyard items.
   C. Some people will be dissatisfied no matter how much they have. They may want more, or they may want to keep what they have forever. One recent television documentary showed several people, motivated by boredom, jetting from New York to Paris for a one-day shopping spree to buy platinum earrings. In Brazil, some people are ordering coffins equipped with deluxe stereos, televisions and other graveyard necessities. The minimum price for these coffins—$45,000.
   D. Some people are never satisfied. No matter how much they have they still want more, or think they can keep what they have forever. One television documentary recently showed several people flying from New York to Paris for the day to buy platinum earrings because they were bored. In Brazil, some people are ordering coffins that cost $45,000 and are equipped with deluxe stereos, televisions and other graveyard necessities.

10. I. A television signal or video signal has three parts.
    II. Its parts are the black-and-white portion, the color portion, and the synchronizing (sync) pulses, which keep the picture stable.
    III. Each video source, whether it's a camera or a video-cassette recorder contains its own generator of these synchronizing pulses to accompany the picture that it's sending in order to keep it steady and straight.
    IV. In order to produce a clean recording, a video-cassette recorder must "lock-up" to the sync pulses that are part of the video it is trying to record, and this effort may be very noticeable if the device does not have gunlock.

    A. There are three parts to a television or video signal: the black-and-white part, the color part, and the synchronizing (sync) pulses, which keep the picture stable. Whether it's a video-cassette recorder or a camera, each video source contains its own pulse that synchronizes and generates the picture it's sending in order to keep it straight and steady. A video-cassette recorder must "lock up" to the sync pulses that are part of the video it's trying to record. If the device doesn't have gunlock, this effort must be very noticeable.
    B. A video signal or television is comprised of three parts: the black-and-white portion, the color portion, and the sync (synchronizing) pulses, which keep the picture stable. Whether it's a camera or a video-cassette recorder, each video source contains its own generator of these synchronizing pulses. These accompany the picture that it's sending in order to keep it straight and steady. A video-cassette recorder must "lock up" to the sync pulses that are part of the video it is trying to record in order to produce a clean recording. This effort may be very noticeable if the device does not have gunlock.
    C. There are three parts to a television or video signal: the color portion, the black-and-white portion, and the sync (synchronizing pulses). These keep the picture stable. Each video source, whether it's a video-cassette recorder or a camera, generates these synchronizing pulses accompanying the picture it's sending in order to keep it straight and steady. If a clean recording is to be produced, a video-cassette recorder must store the sync pulses that are part of the video it is trying to record. This effort may not be noticeable if the device does not have gunlock.
    D. A television signal or video signal has three parts: the black-and-white portion, the color portion, and the synchronizing (sync) pulses. It's the sync pulses which keep the picture stable, which accompany it and keep it steady and straight. Whether it's a camera or a video-cassette recorder, each video source contains its own generator of these synchronizing pulses. To produce a clean recording, a video-cassette recorder must "lock up" to the sync pulses that are part of the video it is trying to record. If the device does not have gunlock, this effort may be very noticeable.

10.____

KEY (CORRECT ANSWERS)

1. C 6. A
2. B 7. B
3. A 8. D
4. B 9. C
5. D 10. D

PREPARING WRITTEN MATERIAL
EXAMINATION SECTION
TEST 1

DIRECTIONS: Each of the sentences in this test may be classified under one of the following four categories:
  A. *Incorrect* because of faulty grammar or sentence structure
  B. *Incorrect* because of faulty punctuation
  C. *Incorrect* because of faulty capitalization
  D. *Correct*

Examine each sentence carefully to determine under which of the above four options it is best classified. Then, in the space at the right, print the capital letter preceding the option which is the BEST of the four suggested above.

(Each incorrect sentence contains but one type of error. Consider a sentence to be correct if it contains none of the types of errors mentioned, even though there may be other correct ways of expressing the same thought.)

1. This fact, together with those brought out at the previous meeting, prove that the schedule is satisfactory to the employees.   1._____

2. Like many employees in scientific fields, the work of bookkeepers and accountants requires accuracy and neatness.   2._____

3. "What can I do for you," the secretary asked as she motioned to the visitor to take a seat.   3._____

4. Our representative, Mr. Charles will call on you next week to determine whether or not your claim has merit.   4._____

5. We expect you to return in the spring; please do not disappoint us.   5._____

6. Any supervisor, who disregards the just complaints of his subordinates, is remiss in the performance of his duty.   6._____

7. Because she took less than an hour for lunch is no reason for permitting her to leave before five o'clock.   7._____

8. "Miss Smith," said the supervisor, "Please arrange a meeting of the staff for two o'clock on Monday."   8._____

9. A private company's vacation and sick leave allowance usually differs considerably from a public agency.   9._____

10. Therefore, in order to increase the efficiency of operations in the department, a report on the recommended changes in procedures was presented to the departmental committee in charge of the program.   10._____

11. We told him to assign the work to whoever was available. 11._____

12. Since John was the most efficient of any other employee in the bureau, he received the highest service rating. 12._____

13. Only those members of the national organization who resided in the middle West attended the conference in Chicago. 13._____

14. The question of whether the office manager has as yet attained, or indeed can ever hope to secure professional status is one which has been discussed for years. 14._____

15. No one knew who to blame for the error which, we later discovered, resulted in a considerable loss of time. 15._____

KEY (CORRECT ANSWERS)

1.	A	6.	B	11.	D
2.	A	7.	A	12.	A
3.	B	8.	C	13.	C
4.	B	9.	A	14.	B
5.	D	10.	D	15.	A

TEST 2

DIRECTIONS: Each of the sentences in this test may be classified under one of the following four categories:
- A. *Incorrect* because of faulty grammar or sentence structure
- B. *Incorrect* because of faulty punctuation
- C. *Incorrect* because of faulty capitalization
- D. *Correct*

1. The National alliance of Businessmen is trying to persuade private businesses to hire youth in the summertime.   1.____

2. The supervisor who is on vacation, is in charge of processing vouchers.   2.____

3. The activity of the committee at its conferences is always stimulating.   3.____

4. After checking the addresses again, the letters went to the mailroom.   4.____

5. The director, as well as the employees, are interested in sharing the dividends.   5.____

KEY (CORRECT ANSWERS)

1. C
2. B
3. D
4. A
5. A

TEST 3

DIRECTIONS: In each of the following groups of sentences, one of the four sentences is faulty in grammar, punctuation, or capitalization. Select the INCORRECT sentence in each case.

1. A. Sailing down the bay was a thrilling experience for me.
   B. He was not consulted about your joining the club.
   C. This story is different than the one I told you yesterday.
   D. There is no doubt about his being the best player.

   1.____

2. A. He maintains there is but one road to world peace.
   B. It is common knowledge that a child sees much he is not supposed to see.
   C. Much of the bitterness might have been avoided if arbitration had been resorted to earlier in the meeting.
   D. The man decided it would be advisable to marry a girl somewhat younger than him.

   2.____

3. A. In this book, the incident I liked least is where the hero tries to put out the forest fire.
   B. Learning a foreign language will undoubtedly give a person a better understanding of his mother tongue.
   C. His actions made us wonder what he planned to do next.
   D. Because of the war, we were unable to travel during the summer vacation.

   3.____

4. A. The class had no sooner become interested in the lesson than the dismissal bell rang.
   B. There is little agreement about the kind of world to be planned at the peace conference.
   C. "Today," said the teacher, "we shall read 'The Wind in the Willows,' I am sure you'll like it.
   D. The terms of the legal settlement of the family quarrel handicapped both sides for many years.

   4.____

5. A. I was so surprised that I was not able to say a word.
   B. She is taller than any other member of the class.
   C. It would be much more preferable if you were never seen in his company.
   D. We had no choice but to excuse her for being late.

   5.____

KEY (CORRECT ANSWERS)

1. C
2. D
3. A
4. C
5. C

TEST 4

DIRECTIONS: In each of the following groups of sentences, one of the four sentences is faulty in grammar, punctuation, or capitalization. Select the INCORRECT sentence in each case.

1. A. Please send me these data at the earliest opportunity.
   B. The loss of their material proved to be a severe handicap.
   C. My principal objection to this plan is that it is impracticable.
   D. The doll had laid in the rain for an hour and was ruined.

2. A. The garden scissors, left out all night in the rain, were in a badly rusted condition.
   B. The girls felt bad about the misunderstanding which had arisen
   C. Sitting near the campfire, the old man told John and I about many exciting adventures he had had.
   D. Neither of us is in a position to undertake a task of that magnitude.

3. A. The general concluded that one of the three roads would lead to the besieged city.
   B. The children didn't, as a rule, do hardly anything beyond what they were told to do.
   C. The reason the girl gave for her negligence was that she had acted on the spur of the moment.
   D. The daffodils and tulips look beautiful in that blue vase.

4. A. If I was ten years older, I should be interested in this work.
   B. Give the prize to whoever has drawn the best picture.
   C. When you have finished reading the book, take it back to the library.
   D. My drawing is as good as or better than yours.

5. A. He asked me whether the substance was animal or vegetable.
   B. An apple which is unripe should not be eaten by a child.
   C. That was an insult to me who am your friend.
   D. Some spy must of reported the matter to the enemy.

6. A. Limited time makes quoting the entire message impossible.
   B. Who did she say was going?
   C. The girls in your class have dressed more dolls this year than we.
   D. There was such a large amount of books on the floor that I couldn't find a place for my rocking chair.

7. A. What with his sleeplessness and his ill health, he was unable to assume any responsibility for the success of the meeting.
   B. If I had been born in February, I should be celebrating my birthday soon.
   C. In order to prevent breakage, she placed a sheet of paper between each of the plates when she packed them.
   D. After the spring shower, the violets smelled very sweet.

8. A. He had laid the book down very reluctantly before the end of the lesson.
    B. The dog, I am sorry to say, had lain on the bed all night.
    C. The cloth was first lain on a flat surface; then it was pressed with a hot iron.
    D. While we were in Florida, we lay in the sun until we were noticeably tanned.

    8.____

9. A. If John was in New York during the recent holiday season, I have no doubt he spent most of the time with his parents.
    B. How could he enjoy the television program; the dog was barking and the baby was crying.
    C. When the problem was explained to the class, he must have been asleep.
    D. She wished that her new dress were finished so that she could go to the party.

    9.____

10. A. The engine not only furnishes power but light and heat as well.
    B. You're aware that we've forgotten whose guilt was established, aren't you?
    C. Everybody knows that the woman made many sacrifices for her children.
    D. A man with his dog and gun is a familiar sight in this neighborhood.

    10.____

KEY (CORRECT ANSWERS)

1.	D	6.	D
2.	C	7.	B
3.	B	8.	C
4.	A	9.	B
5.	D	10.	A

TEST 5

DIRECTIONS: Each of Questions 1 through 5 consists of a sentence which may be classified appropriately under one of the following four categories:
- A. *Incorrect* because of faulty grammar
- B. *Incorrect* because of faulty punctuation
- C. *Incorrect* because of faulty spelling
- D. *Correct*

Examine each sentence carefully. Then, print in the space at the right the letter preceding the category which is the BEST of the four suggested above
(Note: Each incorrect sentence contains only one type of error. Consider a sentence correct if it contains no errors, although there may be other correct ways of writing the sentence.)

1. Of the two employees, the one in our office is the most efficient. 1.____

2. No one can apply or even understand, the new rules and regulations. 2.____

3. A large amount of supplies were stored in the empty office. 3.____

4. If an employee is occassionally asked to work overtime, he should do so willingly. 4.____

5. It is true that the new procedures are difficult to use but, we are certain that you will learn them quickly. 5.____

6. The office manager said that he did not know who would be given a large allotment under the new plan. 6.____

7. It was at the supervisor's request that the clerk agreed to postpone his vacation. 7.____

8. We do not believe that it is necessary for both he and the clerk to attend the conference. 8.____

9. All employees, who display perseverance, will be given adequate recognition. 9.____

10. He regrets that some of us employees are dissatisfied with our new assignments. 10.____

11. "Do you think that the raise was merited," asked the supervisor? 11.____

12. The new manual of procedure is a valuable supplament to our rules and regulations. 12.____

13. The typist admitted that she had attempted to pursuade the other employees to assist her in her work. 13.____

2 (#5)

14. The supervisor asked that all amendments to the regulations be handled by you and I.   14.____

15. The custodian seen the boy who broke the window.   15.____

KEY (CORRECT ANSWERS)

1.	A	6.	D	11.	B
2.	B	7.	D	12.	C
3.	A	8.	A	13.	C
4.	C	9.	B	14.	A
5.	B	10.	D	15.	A

FLOWCHARTING

When you program a computer, you must first think through what you want to get done. It is necessary to take small organized steps. The ordering of your thoughts is called an *algorithm.* It is a step-by-step process to complete a certain task.

For instance, imagine that you are looking for a new job. You need a plan of action. Your algorithm:

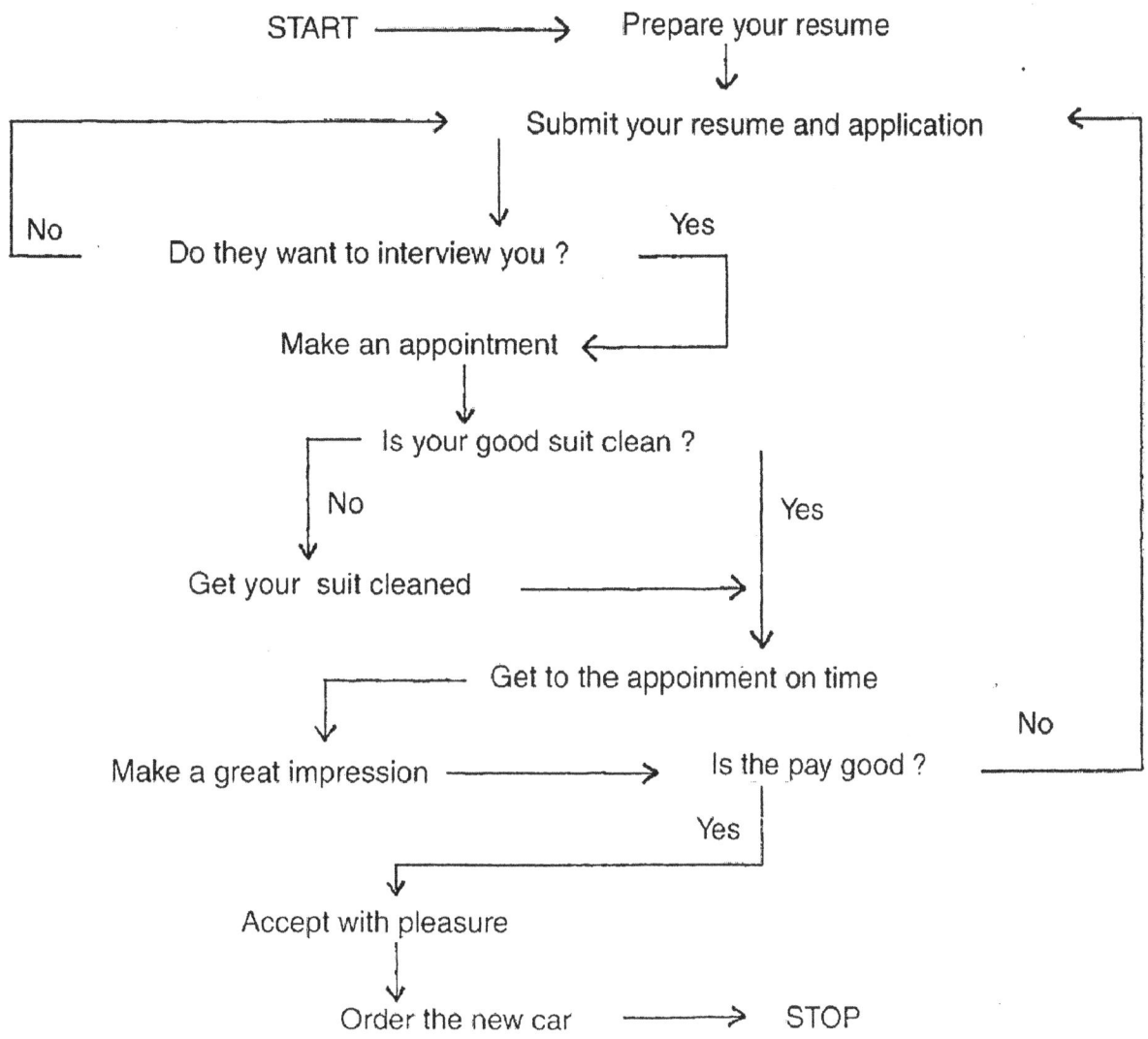

This is the flowchart that goes with your algorithm. Compare them. Note the use of shapes for each step. These are symbols.

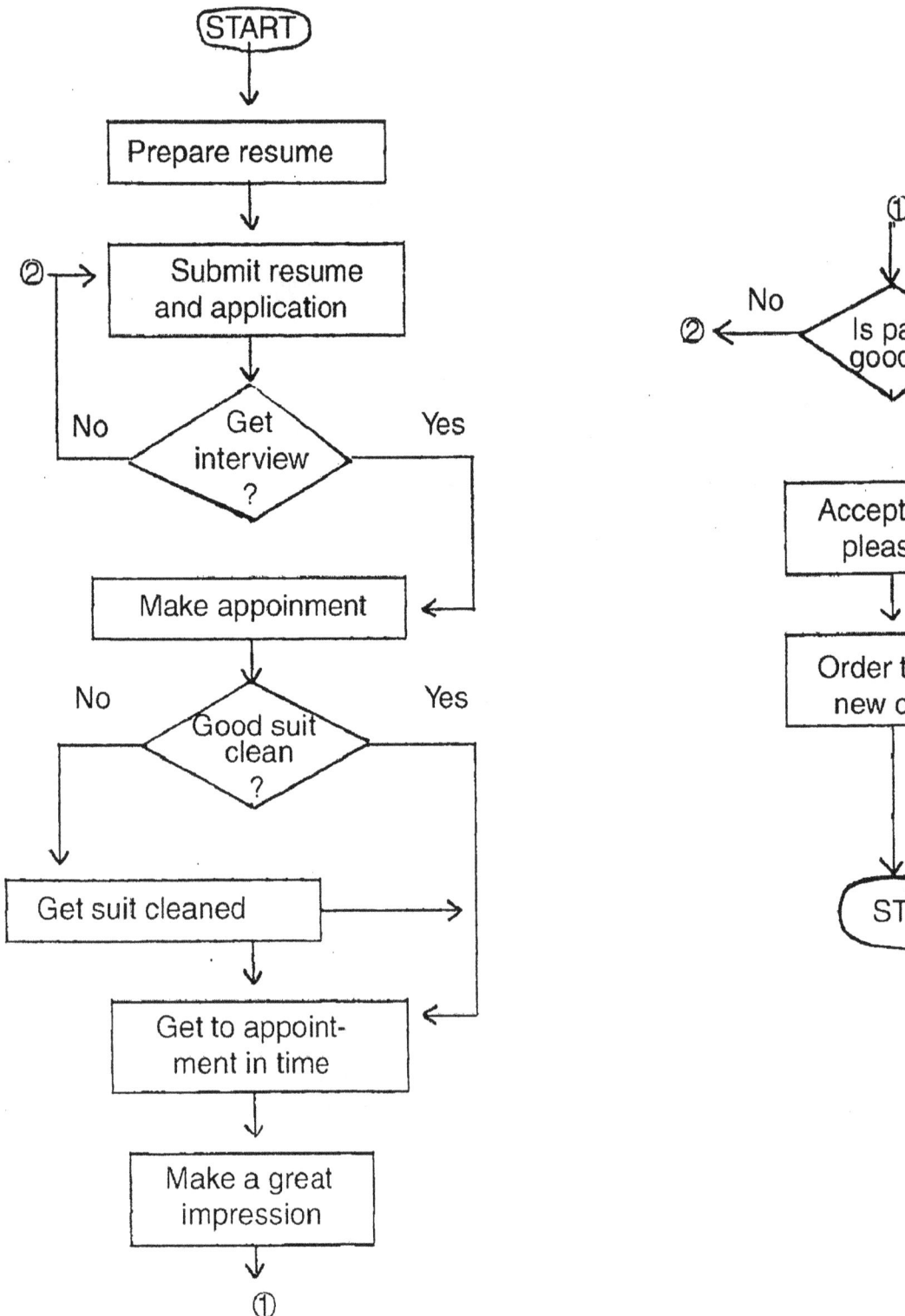

FLOWCHART SYMBOLS make flowcharts uniform and easier to read:

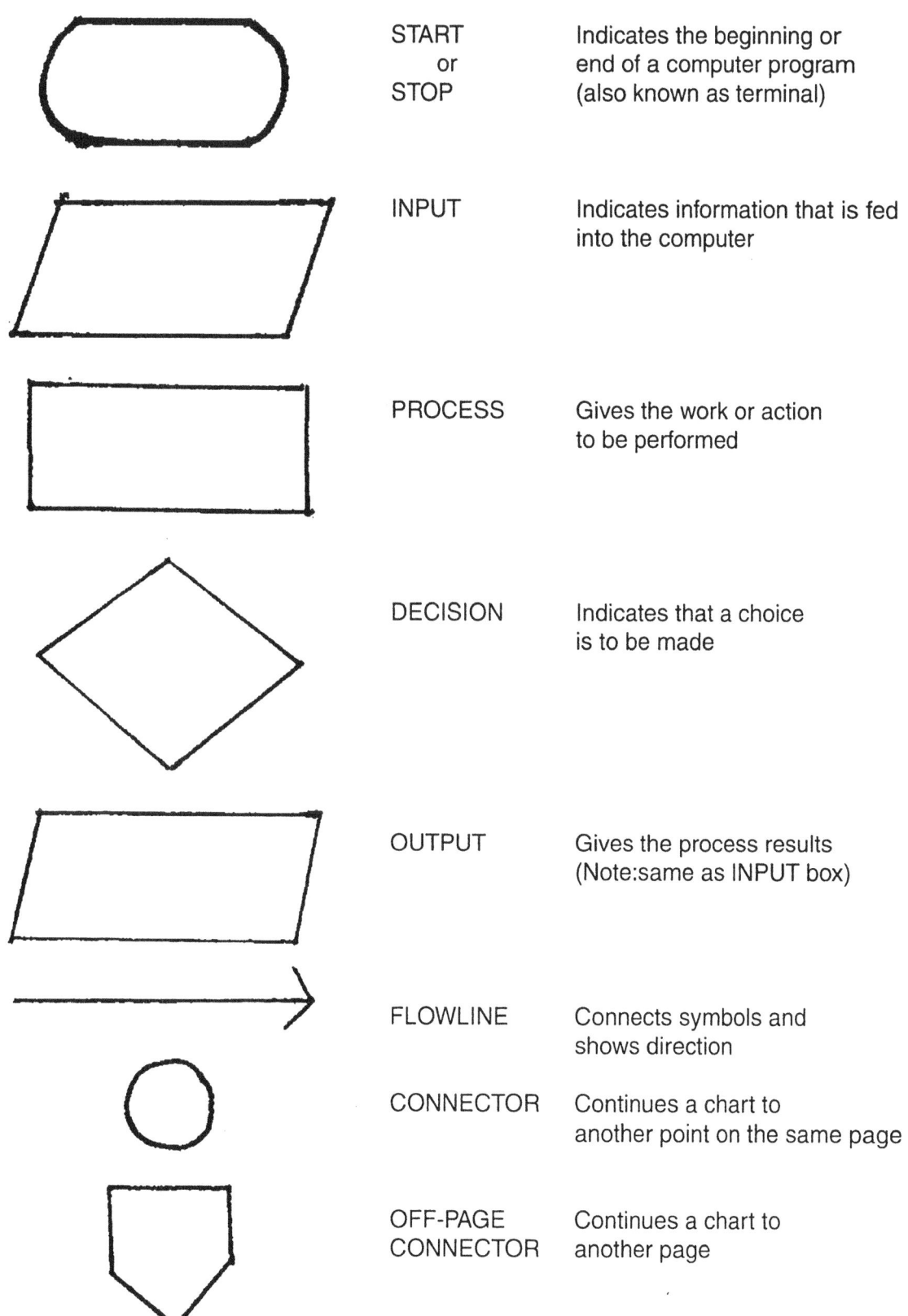

POINTS TO REMEMBER:

An <u>OVAL</u> means the beginning and end of a flowchart; it indicates the terminal points. If you trace it, you will see that one "flowline leads out from START and into STOP.

A <u>PARALLELOGRAM</u> has two purposes, to show input and to show output. Input is information given to the computer. Information gotten from the computer is called output and is also put into a parallelogram. A parallelegram should have one line leading in and one line leading out.

A <u>RECTANGLE</u> represents work done. One task is presented in each box. It will always have one flowline leading in and one leading out.

A <u>DIAMOND</u> represents a decision. It is always phrased as a question which can be answered yes or no. A diamond will have one flowline leading in and two leading out, one marked YES and one marked NO.

A <u>LINE</u> with arrows indicates the direction of the flowchart. These <u>FLOWLINES</u> are always vertical or horizontal and meet each other at right angles. They must <u>never</u> cross each other.

A <u>CIRCLE</u> is used when the flowchart does not fit in the space. One circle has a number which corresponds to another circle on the sane page.

A <u>PENTAGON</u> means that a flowchart will be continued on the next page. The number put in the first pentagon matches the number in a second pentagon found on the following page.

NOTE: Flowcharts should follow a top-to-bottom and left-to-right progression a's much as possible.

Once the job is yours, a flowchart such as the one below may be used to determine what your weekly paycheck is.

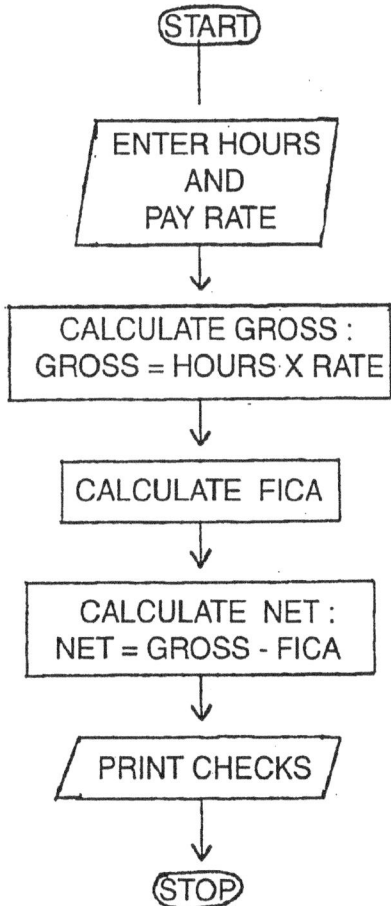

This is a very simple program flowchart, but may be all that is necessary to show the basic procedure. Note the two parallelograms and how their messages differ from those of the rectangles. A programmer might then take this and expand it to show other things — how FICA is determined, for example. You might want to try this if you know the formula for calculating FICA.

Below you will see three flowcharts which are used to solve math problems. The first is an incomplete chart for finding the average of five numbers. The second computes the batting average (B) of a baseball player, given his at-bats (A) and his hits (H). The third determines whether a given number is positive or negative. Complete each by enclosing the steps with the correct symbols and connecting with arrows. Since page 7 gives you the answers, you might want to fold the booklet over or cover the page as you are working to keep from looking at it.

6

#1	#2	#3
START	START	START
ENTER 29,467, 53,902,84	ENTER H, A	AENTER X=50,Y=30
8=29+467+53+902+84	B=H/A	D=X-Y
A=S/5	PRINT B	D>0? (YES / NO)
PRINT A	STOP	PRINT NEGATIVE NUMBER
STOP		PRINT POSITIVE NUMBER
		STOP

Did your charts look like this? If so, great! If not, review pages 3-4. You may be wondering why there is an option to print negative number when the answer is obviously positive. Both options are needed in order to cover all variations of a problem. What if this were a *real* program and it had to handle a problem in which D = Y - X? Then the answer would have been 30-50, or -20.

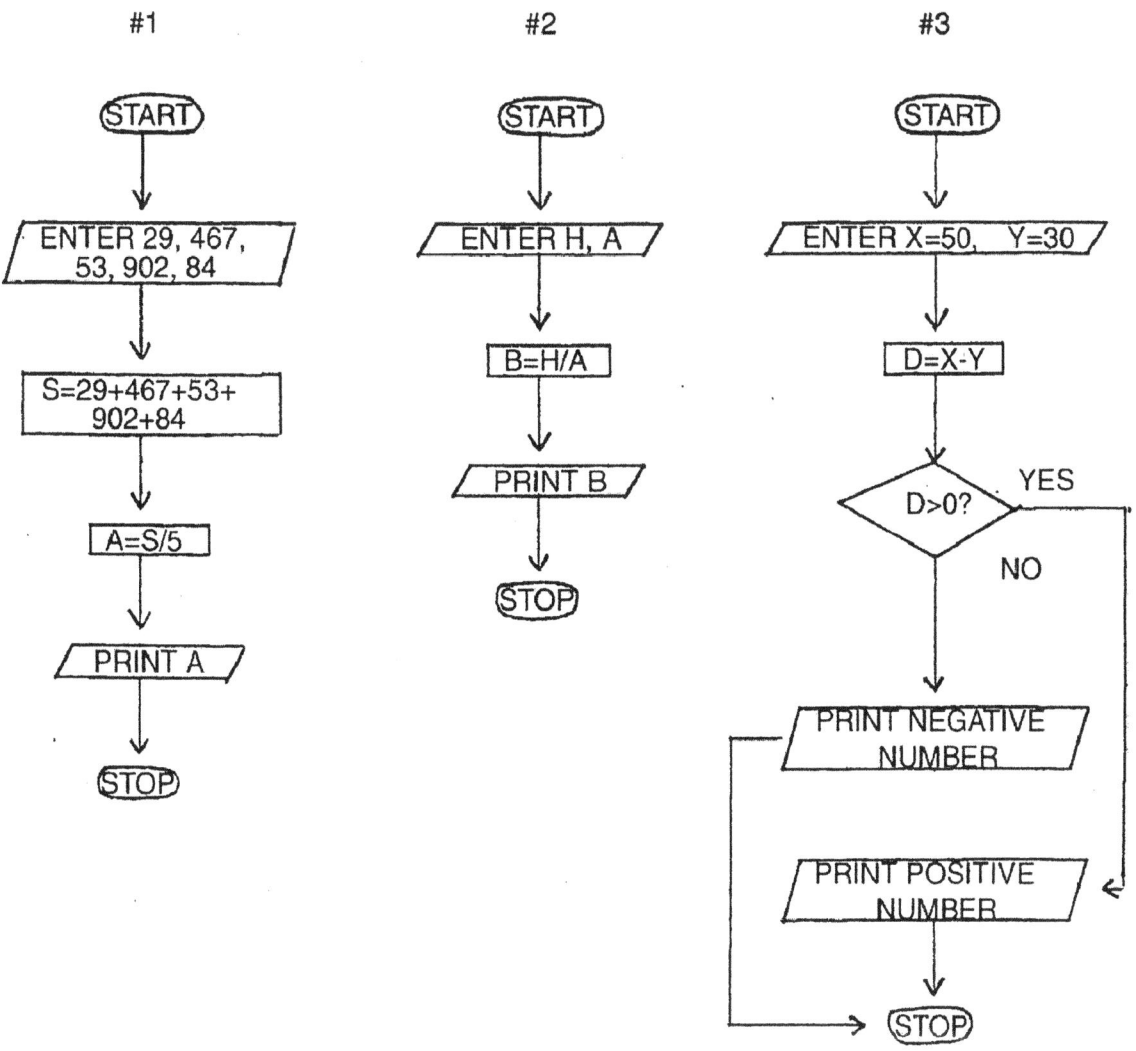

LOOPS:

A loop in a flowchart comes out of a decision box and enables you to return to an earlier point in the chart. To understand the use of the loop, let's look back at the flowchart for job-hunting which was on page 2. There are two loops represented by this flowchart.

The first came out of the diamond-shaped decision box reading *Get interview?* If the answer was *Yes,* you proceeded to make an appointment. If *No,* you *looped* back up to an earlier point and continued the job-hunt by submitting resume and application to another possible employer.

The second loop came from a *No* response to the decision box, *Is pay good?* When you decided *Yes,* the pay was good, you proceeded to accept the job. If you decided *No,* the pay was not good, you returned to an earlier point, submitting your resume and application elsewhere. The flowchart then guided you to repeat the same steps you had taken before. (NOTE:, Loops always flow from, decisions, symbolized in this guide by diamond-shaped boxes, and always return you to an earlier point. Understanding this simple process will help you trace through and understand the most complex flowchart.)

The flowchart that follows shows how to divide a number between 10 and 100 by a number that is less than 10. Study it and then answer the following:

1. This flowchart shows how many loops?

2. What decision is made first?

3. What should you do if the answer is *Yes?*

4. What should you do if the answer is *No?*

5. What is the second decision?

6. What should you do if the answer is *No?*

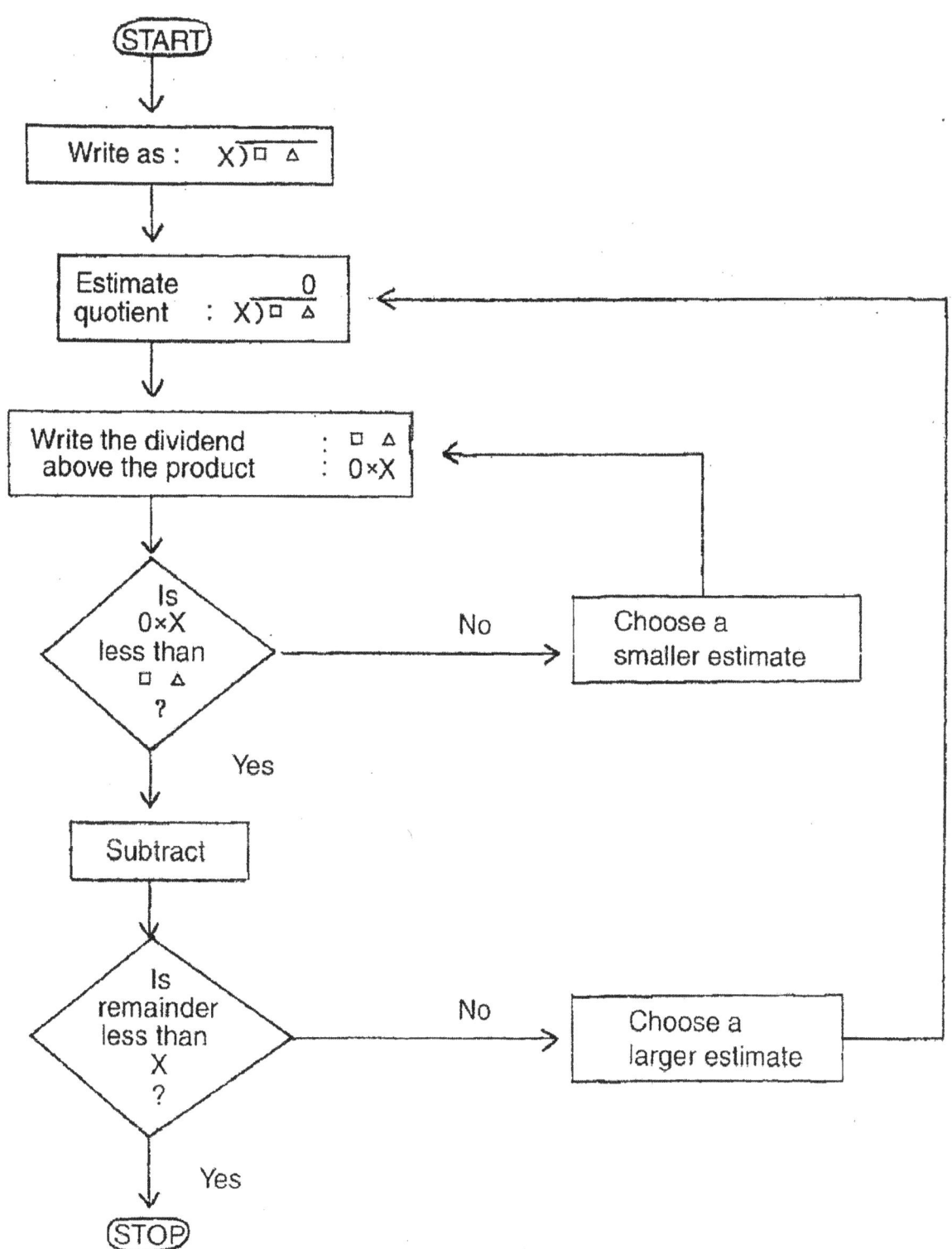

On the following page is an old, almost classic example of flowcharting, which has been titled *How to Get to Work in the Morning.* Use it to answer the questions that follow below. Answers to these questions can be found on the last page of this section.

7. Look at point ⓐ Does this represent a loop? Why or why not?

8. Bow many loops do you find in the chart? Do all the decision boxes in the chart produce loops? How can you tell?

9. What is the first decision? 10. If *Yes,* what do you do?

11. Look at the box that contains ⓑ. Could that box read *How cold?* Why or why not?

12. Which step comes next if the answer at point ⓒ is *No?*

13. If the answer to the step at point ⓓ is *Yes,* what happens?

14. How many times does someone who is married more than 5 years get kissed?

15. How many times does a newlywed get kissed?

16. If point ⓓ had to be located on another page because of space limitations, what should Ⓐ be changed to?

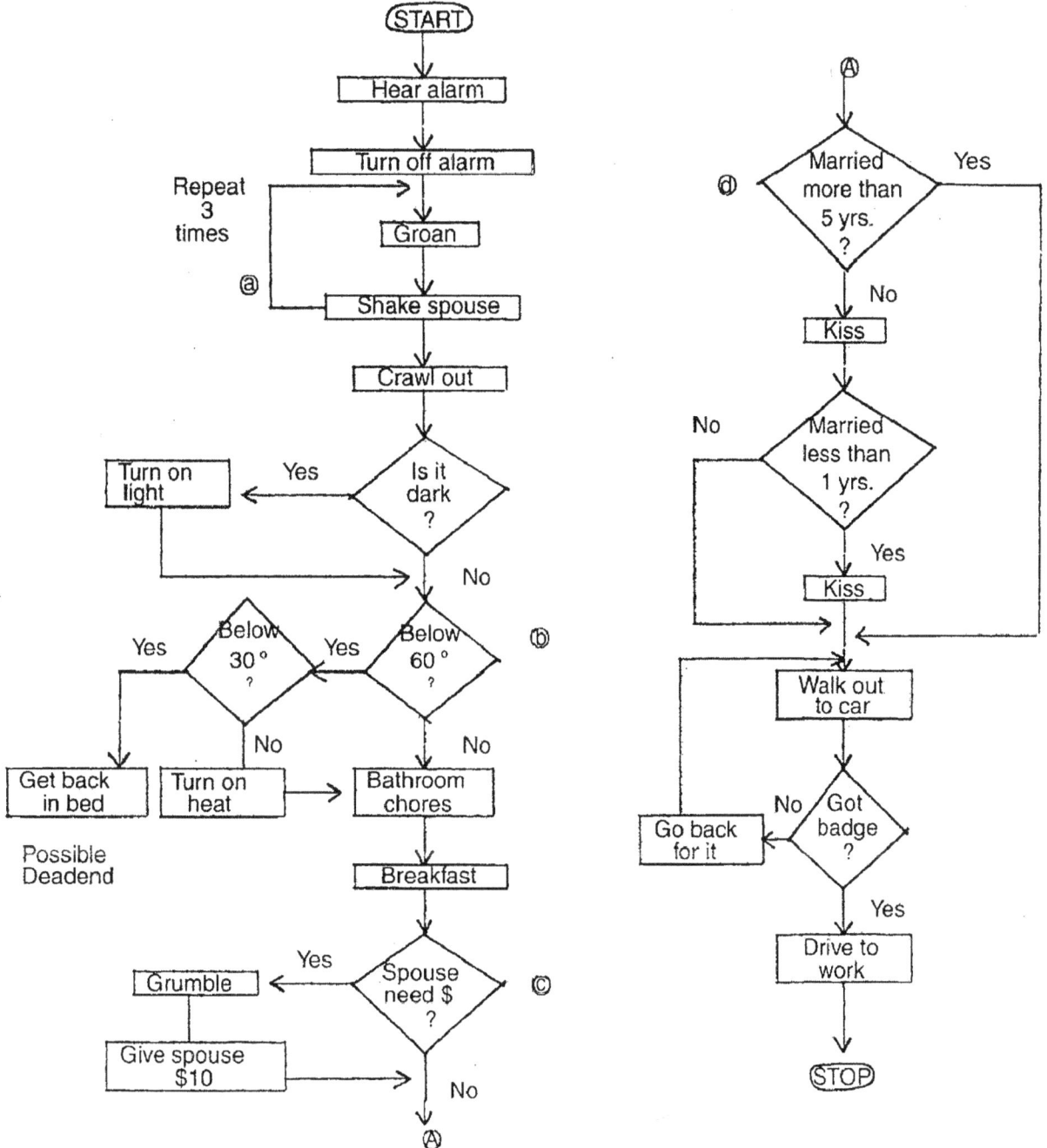

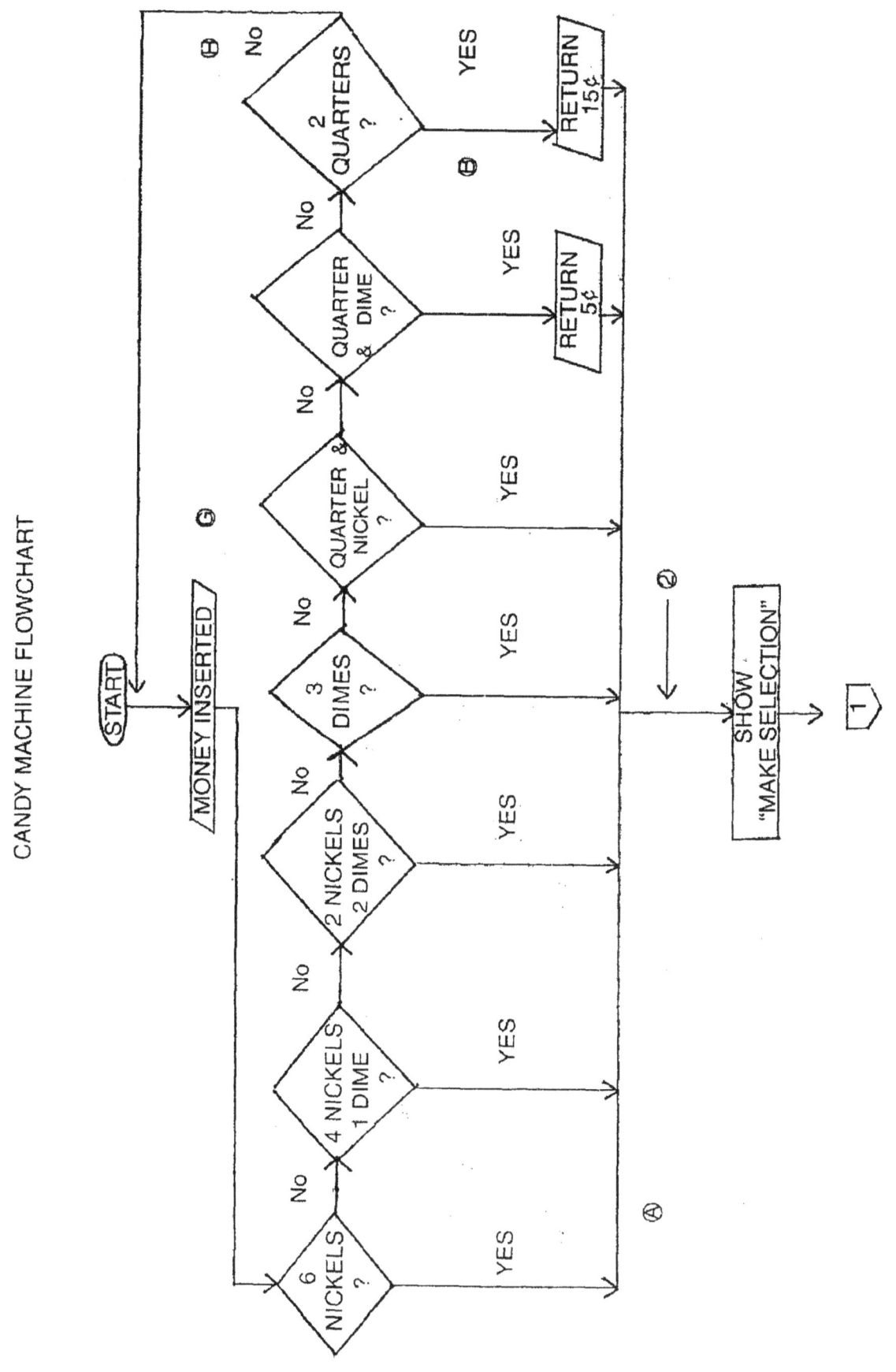

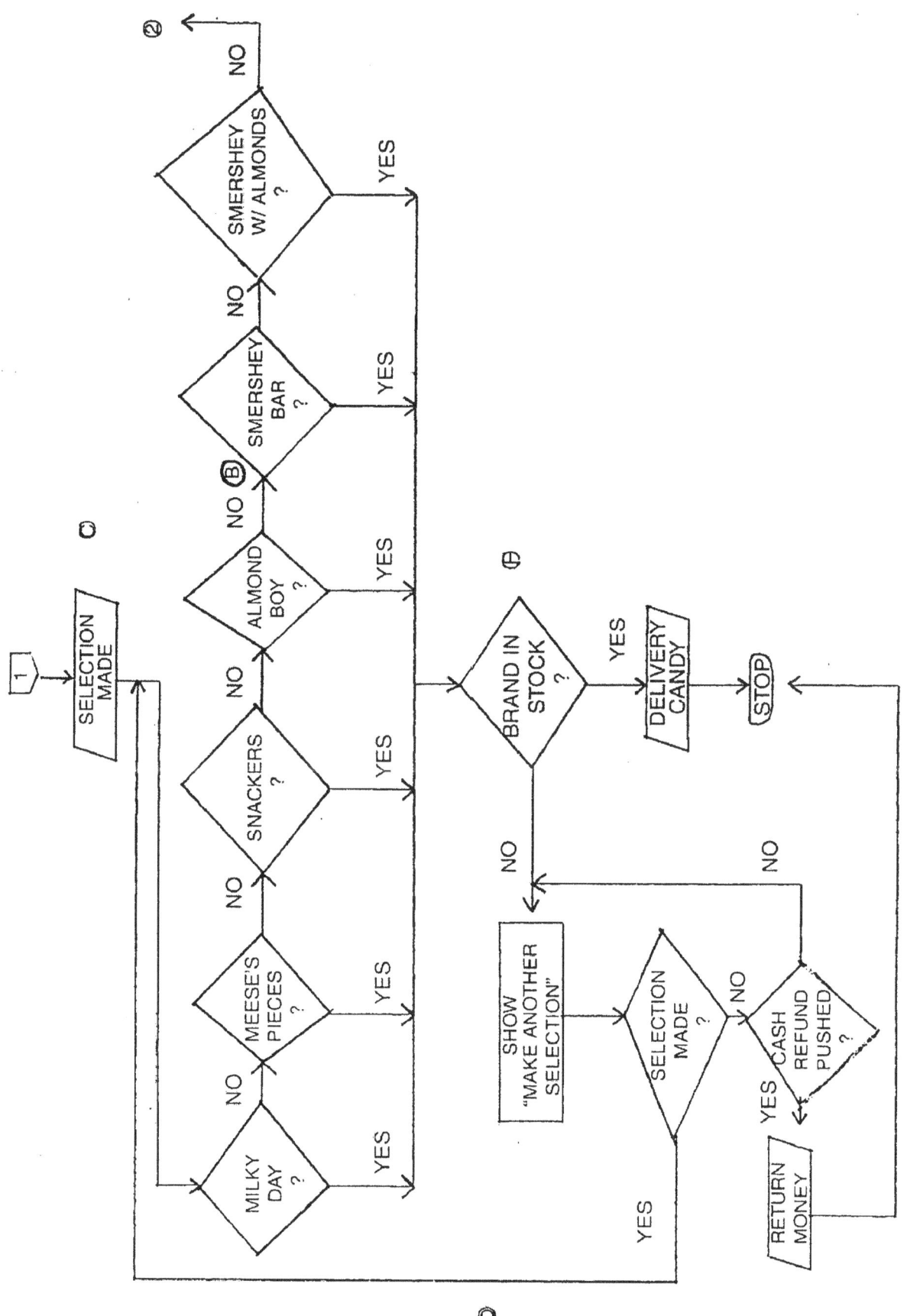

Please study the flowchart for a candy vending machine, then answer the following questions. The answers are at the end of the section.

17. How many brands of candy are available?

18. What is the price of each?

19. What coins may be used?

20. At point Ⓐ, what is the next function?

21. At point Ⓑ what is the next function?

22. Why is point Ⓒ a parallelogram?

23. What three steps immediately preceded point Ⓓ ?

24. If one were to reach point Ⓗ what would that MOST likely mean?

25. What might we call point Ⓓ?

26. At point Ⓔ what brands have been eliminated as selection options?

27. At point Ⓔ, what brands are still selection options?

28. Why is the box at Ⓕ a diamond shape?

29. What does a *Yes* decision at Ⓕ lead to?

30. Name two indicated input points.

31. Name two output boxes.

KEY (CORRECT ANSWERS)

ANSWERS TO QUESTIONS 1-6.

1. Two.

2. Is OxX (the product) less than ?? (the dividend)?

3. Subtract the product from the dividend.

4. *Choose a smaller estimate* and go back to *Write the dividend ?? above the product* OxK to then see if the product is less than the dividend. In other words, you repeat the steps as the loop indicates.

5. *Is the remainder less than* X *(the divisor)?*

6. *Choose a larger estimate* and loop back to repeat the steps as the arrows indicate. You go all the way back to the rectangle immediately preceding the first decision box.

NOTE: Now look back at the flowchart again. See that the lines forming the loops never intersect (cross) each other.

ANSWERS TO *HOW TO GET TO WORK IN THE MORNING*

7. No, point ⓐ doesn't represent a loop. You know this because it doesn't flow from a decision box, a diamond-shaped box that requires a *Yes* or *No* answer.

8. There is only one loop in the chart. No, all the decision boxes in the chart don't produce loops. Only once does it come from a decision box <u>and</u> direct you <u>back</u> to repeat steps. This is at *Got badge?* Remember, loops refer you back to an earlier part in the chart. The only other item that looks like a loop is from *Shake spouse*. It's not a loop, however, it's a way of telling you to repeat an action without taking up space.

9. *Is it dark?* is the first decision.

10. If the answer is *Yes,* then you should *Turn on light.*

11. No, because decision boxes must be able to be answered *Yes* or *No* <u>only</u>.

12. The next step is point ⓓ, *Married more than 5 years?*

13. If the answer to the step at point ⓓ your car. is *Yes,* you walk out to

14. Someone who is married more than 5 years doesn't get kissed at all.

15. A newlywed gets kissed twice.

16. Under these circumstances, Ⓐ should be changed to ⌂A⌂ ; it would become an *off-page connector*.

ANSWERS TO THE *CANDY MACHINE FLOWCHART*

17. 6

18. 30 cents

19. Quarters, nickels and dimes

20. Show *make selection*

21. *Return 15¢*

22. It's a parallelogram because that shape signals input. We are assuming that a candy machine is a computer. In that case, the *keyboard* is the knobs or buttons that are pushed to make a selection or to get a refund. The *keyboard operator* is any person who comes to buy candy. He/she *enters* the data (the selection or the money), and so this is considered input.

23. (1) The selection made was not in stock.
    (2) The consumer was signaled to make another selection.
    (3) Another selection was made.

24. The *operator* did not put in enough money, he or she put in the wrong coins or wrong combination of coins, or the machine is out of order. By the time we get to point Ⓗ, all likely, possible combinations of the coins that will be taken have been exhausted. The flaw here is that there is no detailed provisio for occurrences like: putting in pennies, or putting in too much money. If the person were to put in three quarters, how would he or she get one back? This flowchart doesn't tell us, and this is a flaw in the algorithm.

25. A loop.

26. Milky Day, Meese's Pieces, Snackers, and Almond Boy.

27. Smershey Bar and Smershey with Almonds.

28. It is a decision box. It asks whether or not the brand is in stock.

29. *Deliver sandy*

30. Ⓖ and Ⓒ

31. *Deliver candy, Return 5¢, Return 15¢,* and/or *Return money*

GLOSSARY OF COMPUTER TERMS

Basic

accessibility
The term accessibility refers to information that can be accessed with fewer or no obstacles for as many people as possible. Developers use accessibility features in websites and software to benefit users with disabilities to use computers through assistive technologies.

artificial intelligence
Artificial intelligence or AI is the ability of a computer to perform tasks related to intelligence and think like humans. This technology can process large amounts of data to recognize patterns and make decisions like humans, as seen in programs like ChatGPT.

API
Also called application programming interface, API is a set of protocols and instructions (written in C++ or JavaScript) to determine how two software components will communicate with each other. It defines the kinds of calls and requests made to locate and retrieve the requested information.

application (app)
An application (often called "app" for short) is a computer program that performs specific functions for an end user or another application (in some cases).

authentication
The process of verification of a user or device before allowing access to the system or resources.

bandwidth
A measurement of the amount of data that can be transmitted over a communications path in a given time. The higher the bandwidth, the greater the volume of data transmitted. It is usually measured in bits per second (bps). Modern networks have speed that is measured in the millions of bits per second (megabits per second, or Mbps) or billions of bits per second (gigabits per second, or Gbps).

blockchain
Blockchain technology is an advanced database mechanism that enables the secure sharing of information. It is also known as distributed ledger technology or DLT. The data is stored in blocks that are lined together in a chain.

boot
Starting up an OS is booting it. If the computer is already running, it is more often called rebooting.

browser
A browser is a program used to browse the web. Some common browsers include Google Chrome, Microsoft Edge, Mozilla Firefox, Brave and Safari.

bug
A bug is a mistake in the design of something, especially software. A really severe bug can cause something to crash.

BYOD
Bring Your Own Device or BYOD is a business policy allowing employees to bring in their personal devices and use them to access company data, e-mail and other resources.

Business Intelligence
Business intelligence or BI is a tool that is used by businesses for data collection, analysis and presentation in a meaningful way to drive the decision-making process.

CAPTCHA
Acronym for Completely Automated Public Turing test to tell Computers and Humans Apart. It is

a test in form of distorted text or images that determines if an online user is really a human or an automated user.

cache
A software or hardware component that temporarily stores data in a computing environment to reduce the data retrieval time for future requests.

chatbot
A chat bot or chatterbox is a computer program that is used for simulating and processing human conversation. It is a form of artificial intelligence (AI) that allows humans to interact with digital devices as if they were communicating with a real person.

chat
Chatting is like e-mail, only it is done instantaneously and can directly involve multiple people at once. Chat is a kind of communication over the Internet that allows real-time transmission of messages between sender and receiver. Chat messages are short to enable the participants to respond quickly.

click
To press a mouse button. When done twice in rapid succession, it is referred to as a double-click.

cloud computing
Refers to storage and access data and programs over the Internet instead of any hard drive. Some common cloud services include Dropbox, iCloud and Google Cloud.

cookie
A piece of data from a website stored within a web browser that a website can retrieve at a later time. It is used throughout a user's session to keep track of usage patterns and preferences.

cursor
A point of attention on the computer screen, often marked with a flashing line or block. Text typed into the computer will usually appear at the cursor.

cybercrime
An illegal activity that involves a network or computer. Some common cybercrimes include identity theft, gaining unauthorized access and network intrusions.

cybersecurity
Measures that are designed to protect information, computer devices or networks from cybercrime.

cyberspace
The world of virtual computers, specifically electronic media, used to facilitate online communication.

data center
A physical facility that is used to house an organization's applications and data. The key components of a data center design include servers, storage systems, firewalls, routers, switches and application-delivery controllers.

database
A database is a collection of data, typically organized to make common retrievals easy and efficient. Some common database programs include Oracle, Sybase, Postgres, Mango DB, Microsoft SQL Server, Redis, Filemaker, Adabas, etc.

decryption
It is the process of converting an encrypted message back to its original form. It is the reverse process of encryption.

desktop
A desktop system is a computer designed to sit in one position on a desk somewhere and not move around. Most general-purpose computers are desktop systems. Calling a system a desktop implies nothing about its platform. Industrial desktop systems are typically called workstations.

directory
Also called "folder," a directory is a collection of files typically created for organizational

purposes. Note that a directory is itself a file, so a directory can generally contain other directories. It differs in this way from a partition.

disk
A disk is a physical object used for storing data. It will not forget its data when it loses power. It is always used in conjunction with a disk drive. Some disks can be removed from their drives, some cannot. Generally it is possible to write new information to a disk in addition to reading data from it, but this is not always the case.

drive
A device for storing and/or retrieving data. Some drives (such as disk drives, zip drives, and tape drives) are typically capable of having new data written to them, but some others (like CD-ROMs or DVD-ROMs) are not. Some drives have random access (like disk drives, zip drives, CD-ROMs, and DVD-ROMs), while others only have sequential access (like tape drives).

e-book
An e-book or electronic book is a digital and non-editable text that is available and displayed on electronic devices (smartphone or tablets). The concept behind an e-book is that it should provide all the functionality of an ordinary book but in a manner that is (overall) less expensive and more environmentally friendly. The actual term e-book is somewhat confusingly used to refer to a variety of things: custom software to play e-book titles, dedicated hardware to play e-book titles, and the e-book titles themselves. Individual e-book titles can be free or commercial (but will always be less expensive than their printed counterparts) and have to be loaded into a player to be read. Players vary wildly in capability level. Basic ones allow simple reading and bookmarking; better ones include various features like hypertext, illustrations, audio, and even limited video. Other optional features allow the user to mark-up sections of text, leave notes, circle or diagram things, highlight passages, program or customize settings, and even use interactive fiction.

email
Email is short for electronic mail. It allows for the transfer of information from one user to others, provided they are hooked up via some sort of network Popular email platforms include Gmail and Yahoo.

encryption
The process of data conversion from readable form into encoded form is called encryption. It is used to hide sensitive information and prevent unauthorized access.

end point
Physical devices that are connected to a computer network such as servers, mobile devices, desktop computers and virtual machines.

end user
An individual who will ultimately use an IT product or service.

file
A file is a unit of (usually named) information stored on a computer.

firewall
A network security device that acts as a barrier to monitor and filter incoming and outgoing network traffic and permits/blocks data packets based on previously established security policies.

firmware
Sort of in-between hardware and software, firmware consists of modifiable programs embedded in hardware. Firmware updates should be treated with care since they can literally destroy the underlying hardware if done improperly. There are also cases where neglecting to apply a firmware update can destroy the underlying hardware, so user beware. Cameras, optical drives, printers, mobile phones, network cards, etc. rely on firmware built into their memory for smooth functioning.

floppy
A once-common type of removable disk. Floppy disks did not hold much data, but most

computers were capable of reading them. They typically held 100 KB to 1.44 MB of data.
format
The manner in which data is stored; its organization. For example, VHS, SVHS, and Beta are three different formats of video tape. They are not 100% compatible with each other, but information can be transferred from one to the other with the proper equipment (but not always without loss; SVHS contains more information than either of the other two). Computer information can be stored in literally hundreds of different formats, and can represent text, sounds, graphics, animations, etc. Computer information can be exchanged via different computer types provided both computers can interpret the format used.
freeware
A type of proprietary software that is available for downloading without charge. Depending on the freeware's copyright, the user may or may not reuse the software.
function keys
On a computer keyboard, the keys that start with an "F" and usually (but not always) found on the top row. They are meant to perform user-defined tasks.
GPS
GPS or Global Positioning System is a radio-based global navigation satellite system that allows the user to determine a location on Earth.
graphics
Anything visually displayed on a computer that is not text.
GUI
A graphical user interface (GUI) is a digital interface through which a user interacts with electronic devices (smartphones, computers) with graphical components such as icons, menus, buttons and other visual indicators. GUI representations are manipulated by mouse, touch screen, finger, stylus, or trackball.
hardware
The physical portion of the computer.
help desk
A help desk is an information and assistance resource that provides technical support for hardware or software. Companies provide help desk support to their customers via a toll-free number, e-mail or website. The goal of a help desk is to help customers troubleshoot issues and guide them to navigate technology properly.
hypertext
A hypertext document is like a text document with the ability to contain pointers to other regions of (possibly other) hypertext documents.
IaaS
Infrastructure as a Service (IaaS) is the most basic cloud-service model that offers computing, storage and networking resources on demand and pay-as-you-go basis.
Internet
The Internet is the world-wide network of computers.
IoT
Internet of Things (IoT) refers to the collective network of connected devices and the technology that facilitates communication between devices and the cloud. IoT includes anything with a sensor that is assigned a unique identifier (UID).
IT infrastructure
Systems that are put in place to facilitate operation and management of IT services and environments. There are two types of IT infrastructure: traditional infrastructure and cloud infrastructure.
keyboard
A keyboard on a computer is almost identical to a keyboard on a typewriter. Computer keyboards will typically have extra keys, however. Some of these keys (common examples include Control, Alt, and Fn) are meant to be used in conjunction with other keys just like shift on

a regular typewriter. Other keys (common examples include Insert, Delete, Home, End, Help, function keys,etc.) are meant to be used independently and often perform editing tasks. Keyboards on different platforms will often look slightly different and have somewhat different collections of keys.

LAN
A local area network (LAN) is a group of connected computing devices that usually share a centralized Internet connection. A LAN may serve 2-3 users in a home or thousands of users in a central office.

language
Computer programs can be written in a variety of different languages. Different languages are optimized for different tasks. Common languages include JavaScript, Python, C#, Rust, Kotlin, Swift, Go and Elixir. Some people classify languages into two categories, higher-level and lower-level. These people would consider assembly language and machine language lower-level languages and all other languages higher-level. In general, higher-level languages can be either interpreted or compiled; many languages allow both, but some are restricted to one or the other. Many people do not consider machine language and assembly language at all when talking about programming languages.

laptop
A laptop is any computer designed for portability with the capability to do most of the same functions as a desktop system. They are battery-powered and typically provide several hours of use between charges. Most laptops run Windows or Apple operating systems, though Google's Chromebook laptop has gained in popularity.

learning management system (LMS)
Software that is developed to create, use, manage, deliver and store online training course content for audience. The primary purpose of an LMS is to simplify the learning process for the organization and keep the knowledge of an audience up to date.

machine learning (ML)
A branch of artificial intelligence (AI) that uses data and algorithms to improve the performance of AI to imitate intelligent human behavior.

malware
Malware, also referred to as malicious software, is a program or file that is designed to disrupt computer systems, networks or servers. Some common types of malware include viruses, worms, Trojan horses, ransomware and spyware.

mail server
A mail server is a dedicated software program that supports electronic mail. It stores incoming mail for distribution to users and forwards outgoing mail. Some common mail servers include Microsoft Exchange, iCloud Mail and Sendmail.

memory
Computer memory is used to temporarily store data. In reality, computer memory is only capable of remembering sequences of zeros and ones, but by utilizing the binary number system it is possible to produce arbitrary rational numbers and through clever formatting all manner of representations of pictures, sounds, and animations. The most common types of memory are RAM, ROM, and flash.

MHz & megahertz
One megahertz is equivalent to 1000 kilohertz, or 1,000,000 hertz. The clock speed of the main processor of many computers is measured in MHz, and is sometimes (quite misleadingly) used to represent the overall speed of a computer. In fact, a computer's speed is based upon many factors, and since MHz only reveals how many clock cycles the main processor has per second (saying nothing about how much is actually accomplished per cycle), it can really only accurately be used to gauge two computers with the same generation and family of processor plus similar configurations of memory, co-processors, and other peripheral hardware.

modem
A modem allows two computers to communicate over ordinary phone lines. It derives its name from modulate / demodulate, the process by which it converts digital computer data back and forth for use with an analog phone line.
monitor
The screen for viewing computer information is called a monitor.
mouse
In computer parlance a mouse can be both the physical object moved around to control a pointer on the screen, and the pointer itself.
multimedia
This originally indicated a capability to work with and integrate various types of things including audio, still graphics, and especially video. Now it is more of a marketing term and has little real meaning.
NC
The term network computer refers to any (usually desktop) computer system that is designed to work as part of a network rather than as a stand-alone machine. This saves money on hardware, software, and maintenance by taking advantage of facilities already available on the network. The term "Internet appliance" is often used interchangeably with NC.
network
A network (as applied to computers) typically means a group of computers working together. It can also refer to the physical wires connecting the computers.
notebook
A notebook is a small laptop with similar price, performance, and battery life.
organizer
An organizer is a tiny computer used primarily to store names, addresses, phone numbers, and date book information. They usually have some ability to exchange information with desktop systems. They are extremely inexpensive but are typically incapable of running any special-purpose applications and are thus of limited use.
OS (Operating System)
The operating system is the program that manages a computer's resources. Commonly used OSs include Ubuntu, Windows, MacOS, Android, and Google ChromeOS.
PaaS
Platform as a Service (PaaS) is a cloud computing model that provides a computing platform including hardware, software, and infrastructure for development, running and management of applications. PaaS frees the developers to install in-house hardware and software to develop or run a new application.
PC
The term personal computer properly refers to any desktop, laptop, or notebook computer system. Its use is inconsistent, though, and some use it to specifically refer Windows-based computers.
PDA
A personal digital assistant is a predecessor of mobile phones and smartphones. It is a small battery-powered computer intended to be carried around by the user rather than left on a desk. It is used to carry out certain functions, including scheduling, organization, translation, etc. PDAs largely became obsolete with the advance and improvement of mobile-phone technology.
phishing
A common type of cyberattack that targets victims through phone calls, email, text messages or other forms of communication. This attack aims to trick the receiver by posing as a trustworthy entity to obtain sensitive information such as credit card details, personally identifiable information and login credentials.
platform
Roughly speaking, a platform represents a computer's family. It is defined by both the processor

type on the hardware side and the OS type on the software side. Computers belonging to different platforms cannot typically run each other's programs (unless the programs are written in a language like Java).

portable
If something is portable it can be easily moved from one type of computer to another. The verb "to port" indicates the moving itself.

printer
A printer is a piece of hardware that will print computer information onto paper.

processor
The processor (also called central processing unit, or CPU) is the part of the computer that actually works with the data and runs the programs. There are two main processor types in common usage today: CISC and RISC. Some computers have more than one processor and are thus called "multiprocessor". This is distinct from multitasking. Advertisers often use megahertz numbers as a means of showing a processor's speed. This is often extremely misleading; megahertz numbers are more or less meaningless when compared across different types of processors.

program
A program is a series of instructions for a computer, telling it what to do or how to behave. The terms "application" and "app" mean almost the same thing (albeit applications generally have GUIs). It is however different from an applet. Program is also the verb that means to create a program, and a programmer is one who programs.

run
Running a program is how it is made to do something. The term "execute" means the same thing.

SaaS
Software as a Service (SaaS) is a cloud-based software delivery model that delivers applications over the Internet. SaaS enables companies to use software on-promise without worrying about installing, renewing and maintaining them.

search engine
A software program or tool that enables the users to search information on the internet. It creates indexes of databases based on titles of files, keywords or full text of files. Google, Baidu and Yahoo are some popular search engines.

SEO
SEO or search engine optimization is the process and practice of improving various aspects of a website to increase its visibility in search engines.

software
The non-physical portion of the computer; the part that exists only as data; the programs. Another term meaning much the same is "code."

spam
Use of electronic messaging systems to send unwanted bulk messages. Different types of spam include phishing emails, email spoofing, tech support scams, malspam, spam calls and spam texts.

spreadsheet
A program used to perform various calculations. It is especially popular for financial applications. Some common spreadsheets include Microsoft Excel and Google Sheets.

Trojan horse
A Trojan horse or Trojan is a type of malware that is designed to disguise itself as legitimate code to perform harmful acts. Once it is inside the network, the attacker can carry out any action that legitimate user could perform such as deleting files, modifying data, exporting files, etc.

troubleshooting
The process of providing technical support that includes identification, planning and resolution of problems, faults or errors within the computer system or software.

user
The operator of a computer.
virtual machine
A virtual machine or VM is a computer resource that is not physical. It uses software instead of a physical computer for running programs and deploying applications. VM software can run operating systems, connect to networks, store data and perform other computational functions. Some popular VM include VMware Workstation, VirtualBox, QEMU, Citrix and VMWare Fusion.
VPN
A virtual private network (VPN) is an encrypted internet connection. A VPN hides actual public IP addresses of the user and tunnels the traffic between user's device and the remote server. The aim of using VPN is to ensure sensitive data is safely transmitted.
WAN
A wide area network or WAN is a type of network that exists over a large geographical area.
Wi-Fi
A wireless technology using radio waves to provide high-speed Internet access.
word processor
A program designed to help with the production of textual documents, like letters and memos. Heavier duty work can be done with a desktop publisher. Some common word processors include Microsoft Word and Google Docs.
workstation
A workstation is an individual computer or group of computers that are used by a single user to accomplish professional tasks. Workstations are useful for development and applications that need moderate amount of computing power and high-quality graphics.
www
The World-Wide-Web refers more or less to all the publicly accessible documents on the Internet. It is used quite loosely, and sometimes indicates only HTML files and sometimes FTP and Gopher files, too. It is also sometimes just referred to as "the web".

Reference

The following are past and present elements of computing and computer systems, to be reviewed for reference purposes. In some cases, the element is no longer relevant to modern computing but is important for the study and understanding of previous computing environments.

a11y
Commonly used to abbreviate the word "accessibility." There are eleven letters between the "a" and the "y".
ADA
An object-oriented language at one point popular for military and some academic software.
AIX
The industrial strength OS designed by IBM to run on PowerPC and x86 based machines. It was a variant of UNIX and was meant to provide more power than OS/2.
AJaX
AJaX is a little like DHTML, but it adds asynchronous communication between the browser and Web site via either XML or JSON to achieve performance that often rivals desktop applications.
AltiVec
AltiVec (also called the "Velocity Engine") was a special extension built into some PowerPC CPUs to provide better performance for certain operations, most notably graphics and sound. It was similar to MMX on the x86 CPUs. Like MMX, it required special software for full performance benefits to be realized.

Amiga
A platform originally created and only produced by Commodore and later owned by Gateway 2000 and produced by it and a few smaller companies. It was historically the first multimedia machine and gave the world of computing many innovations. Many music videos were created on Amigas, and a few television series and movies had their special effects generated on Amigas. Also, Amigas were readily synchronized with video cameras, so typically when a computer screen appears on television or in a movie and it is not flickering wildly, it is probably an Amiga in disguise. Many coin-operated arcade games were really Amigas packaged in stand-up boxes.

AmigaOS
The OS used by Amigas. AmigaOS combined the functionality of an OS and a window manager and was fully multitasking. AmigaOS boasted a pretty good selection of games (many arcade games are in fact written on Amigas) but had limited driver support. AmigaOS ran on 68xx, Alpha, and PowerPC based machines.

Apple II
The Apple II computer sold millions of units and is generally considered to have been the first home computer with a 1977 release date. It is based on the 65xx family of processors. The earlier Apple I was only available as a build-it-yourself kit.

AppleScript
A scripting language for Mac OS computers. It is used for basic calculations, text processing and processing complex tasks.

applet
An applet differs from an application in that is not meant to be run stand-alone but rather with the assistance of another program, usually a browser.

Aqua
The default window manager for Mac OS X.

Archie
Archie was a system for searching through FTP archives for particular files. It tends not to be used too much anymore as more general modern search engines are significantly more capable.

ARM
An ARM is a RISC processor invented by Advanced RISC Machines. ARMs are different from most other processors in that they were not designed to maximize speed but rather to maximize speed per power consumed. Thus ARMs found most of their use on hand-held machines and PDAs. A few different OSes run on ARM based machines including Newton OS, JavaOS, Windows CE and Linux. The Cortex-X4 is the fastest ARM CPU ever built.

ASCII
The ASCII character set is the most popular one in common use. People will often refer to a bare text file without complicated embedded format instructions as an ASCII file, and such files can usually be transferred from one computer system to another with relative ease. Unfortunately, there are a few minor variations of it that pop up here and there, and if you receive a text file that seems subtly messed up with punctuation marks altered or upper and lower case reversed, you are probably encountering one of the ASCII variants. It is usually fairly straightforward to translate from one ASCII variant to another, though. The ASCII character set is seven bit while pure binary is usually eight bit, so transferring a binary file through ASCII channels will result in corruption and loss of data. Note also that the ASCII character set is a subset of the Unicode character set.

ASK
A protocol for an infrared communications port on a device. It predates the IrDA compliant infrared communications protocol and is not compatible with it. Many devices with infrared communications support both, but some only support one or the other.

assembly language
Assembly language is essentially machine language that has had some of the numbers

replaced by somewhat easier to remember mnemonics in an attempt to make it more human-readable. The program that converts assembly language to machine language is called an assembler. While assembly language predates FORTRAN, it is not typically what people think of when they discuss computer languages.

authoring system
Any GUIs method of designing new software can be called an authoring system. Any computer language name with the word "visual" in front of it is probably a version of that language built with some authoring system capabilities.

AWK
AWK is an interpreted language developed in 1977 by Aho, Weinberger, & Kernighan. It gets its name from its creators' initials. It was not particularly fast, but it was designed for creating small throwaway programs rather than full-blown applications -- it is designed to make the writing of the program fast, not the program itself. It was quite portable with versions existing for numerous platforms, including a free GNU version. Plus, virtually every version of UNIX in the world came with AWK built-in.

BASIC
The Beginners' All-purpose Symbolic Instruction Code is a computer language developed by Kemeny & Kurtz in 1964.

baud
A measure of communications speed, used typically for modems indicating how many bits per second can be transmitted.

BBS
A bulletin board system was a computer that could be directly connected to via modem and provided various services like e-mail, chatting, newsgroups, and file downloading. BBSs waned in popularity with the rise of Internet access.

BeOS
A lightweight OS available for both PowerPC and x86 based machines. It is often referred to simply as "Be".

beta
A beta version of something is not yet ready for prime time but still possibly useful to related developers and other interested parties. Expect beta software to crash more than properly released software does. Traditionally beta versions (of commercial software) are distributed only to selected testers who are often then given a discount on the proper version after its release in exchange for their testing work. Beta versions of non-commercial software are more often freely available to anyone who has an interest.

binary
There are two meanings for binary in common computer usage. The first is the name of the number system in which there are only zeros and ones. This is important to computers because all computer data is ultimately a series of zeros and ones, and thus can be represented by binary numbers. The second is an offshoot of the first; data that is not meant to be interpreted through a common character set (like ASCII) is typically referred to as binary data. Pure binary data is typically eight bit data, and transferring a binary file through ASCII channels without prior modification will result in corruption and loss of data. Binary data can be turned into ASCII data via uucoding or bcoding.

bit
A bit can either be on or off; one or zero. All computer data can ultimately be reduced to a series of bits. The term is also used as a (very rough) measure of sound quality, color quality, and even processor capability by considering the fact that series of bits can represent binary numbers. For example (without getting too technical), an eight bit image can contain at most 256 distinct colors while a sixteen bit image can contain at most 65,536 distinct colors.

bitmap
A bitmap is a simplistic representation of an image on a computer, simply indicating whether or

not pixels are on or off, and sometimes indicating their color. Often fonts are represented as bitmaps. The term "pixmap" is sometimes used similarly; typically when a distinction is made, pixmap refers to color images and bitmap refers to monochrome images.

blog

Short for web log, a blog is a website or page containing periodic (usually frequent) posts. Blogs are usually syndicated via either some type of RSS or Atom and often supports TrackBacks. It is not uncommon for blogs to function much like newspaper columns. A blogger is someone who writes for and maintains a blog.

boolean

Boolean algebra is the mathematics of base two numbers. Since base two numbers have only two values, zero and one, there is a good analogy between base two numbers and the logical values "true" & "false". In common usage, booleans are therefore considered to be simple logical values like true & false and the operations that relate them, most typically "and", "or" and "not". Since everyone has a basic understanding of the concepts of true & false and basic conjunctions, everyone also has a basic understanding of boolean concepts -- they just may not realize it.

byte

A byte is a grouping of bits. It is typically eight bits, but there are those who use non-standard byte sizes. Bytes are usually measured in large groups, and the term "kilobyte" (often abbreviated as K) means one-thousand twenty-four (1024) bytes; the term "megabyte" (often abbreviated as M) means one-thousand twenty-four (1024) K; the term gigabyte (often abbreviated as G) means one-thousand twenty-four (1024) M; and the term "terabyte" (often abbreviated as T) means one-thousand twenty-four (1024) G. Memory is typically measured in kilobytes or megabytes, and disk space is typically measured in megabytes or gigabytes. Note that the multipliers here are 1024 instead of the more common 1000 as would be used in the metric system. This is to make it easier to work with the binary number system.

bytecode

Sometimes computer languages that are said to be either interpreted or compiled are in fact neither and are more accurately said to be somewhere in between. Such languages are compiled into bytecode which is then interpreted on the target system. Bytecode tends to be binary but will work on any machine with the appropriate runtime environment (or virtual machine) for it.

C

C is one of the most popular computer languages in the world, and quite possibly *the* most popular. It is a compiled language widely supported on many platforms. It tends to be more portable than FORTRAN but less portable than Java; it has been standardized by ANSI as "ANSI C" -- older versions are called either "K&R C" or "Kernighan and Ritchie C" (in honor of C's creators), or sometimes just "classic C". Fast and simple, it can be applied to all manner of general purpose tasks. C compilers are made by several companies, but the free GNU version (gcc) is still considered one of the best. Newer C-like object-oriented languages include both Java and C++.

C#

C# is a compiled object-oriented language based heavily on C++ with some Java features.

C++

C++ is a compiled object-oriented language. Based heavily on C, C++ is nearly as fast and can often be thought of as being just C with added features. It is currently probably the second most popular object-oriented language, but it has the drawback of being fairly complex -- the much simpler but somewhat slower Java is probably the most popular object-oriented language. Note that C++ was developed independently of the somewhat similar Objective-C; it is however related to Objective-C++.

C64/128

The Commodore 64 computer was a massively successful model of computer with estimated tens of millions units sold. Its big brother, the Commodore 128, was not quite as popular but still sold several million units. Both units sported ROM-based BASIC and used it as a default "OS". The C128 also came with CP/M (it was a not-often-exercised option on the C64). In their later days they were also packaged with GEOS. Both are based on 65xx family processors.

chain
Some computer devices support chaining, the ability to string multiple devices in a sequence plugged into just one computer port. Often, but not always, such a chain will require some sort of terminator to mark the end. For an example, a SCSI scanner may be plugged into a SCSI CD-ROM drive that is plugged into a SCSI hard drive that is in turn plugged into the main computer. For all these components to work properly, the scanner would also have to have a proper terminator in use. Device chaining has been around a long time, and it is interesting to note that C64/128 serial devices supported it from the very beginning.

character set
Since in reality all a computer can store are series of zeros and ones, representing common things like text takes a little work. The solution is to view the series of zeros and ones instead as a sequence of bytes, and map each one to a particular letter, number, or symbol. The full mapping is called a character set. The most popular character set is commonly referred to as ASCII. The second most popular character set is Unicode

COBOL
The Common Business Oriented Language is a language developed back in 1959. While it was relatively portable, it was disliked by many professional programmers simply because COBOL programs tended to be physically longer than equivalent programs written in almost any other language in common use.

compiled
If a program is compiled, its original human-readable source has been converted into a form more easily used by a computer prior to it being run. Such programs will generally run more quickly than interpreted programs, because time was pre-spent in the compilation phase. A program that compiles other programs is called a compiler.

compression
It is often possible to remove redundant information or capitalize on patterns in data to make a file smaller. Usually when a file has been compressed, it cannot be used until it is uncompressed. Image files are common exceptions, though, as many popular image file formats have compression built-in.

cookie
A cookie is a small file that a web page on another machine writes to your personal machine's disk to store various bits of information. Many people strongly detest cookies and the whole idea of them, and most browsers allow the reception of cookies to be disabled or at least selectively disabled. Sites that maintain shopping carts or remember a reader's last position have legitimate uses for cookies. Sites without such functionality that still spew cookies with distant (or worse, non-existent) expiration dates should perhaps be treated with a little caution.

crash
If a bug in a program is severe enough, it can cause that program to crash, or to become inoperable without being restarted. On machines that are not multitasking, the entire machine will crash and have to be rebooted. On machines that are only partially multitasking the entire machine will sometimes crash and have to be rebooted. On machines that are fully multitasking, the machine should never crash and require a reboot.

crippleware
Crippleware is a variant of shareware that will either self-destruct after its trial period or has built-in limitations to its functionality that get removed after its purchase.

CSS
Cascading style sheets are used in conjunction with HTML and XHTML to define the layout of web pages. While CSS is how current web pages declare how they should be displayed, it

tends not to be supported well (if at all) by ancient browsers.
desktop publisher
A program for creating newspapers, magazines, books, etc. Some common desktop publishing programs include Adobe InDesign, Canva, Affinity Publisher and Microsoft Publisher.
DHTML
Dynamic HTML is simply the combined use of both CSS and JavaScript together in the same document; a more extreme form is called AJaX. Note that DHTML is quite different from the similarly named DTML.
dict
A protocol used for looking up definitions across a network (in particular the Internet).
digital camera
A digital camera looks and behaves like a regular camera, except instead of using film, it stores the image it sees in memory as a file for later transfer to a computer. Many digital cameras offer additional storage besides their own internal memory; a few sport some sort of disk but the majority utilize some sort of flash card. Digital cameras were eventually integrated into mobile phones and are now a dominant element of smartphone technology.
DNS
Domain name service is the means by which a name (like www.saugus.net or ftp.saugus.net) gets converted into a real Internet address that points to a particular machine.
DoS
In a denial of service attack, many individual (usually compromised) computers are used to try and simultaneously access the same public resource with the intent of overburdening it so that it will not be able to adequately serve its normal users.
DOS
A disk operating system manages disks and other system resources. Sort of a subset of OSes, sort of an archaic term for the same. MS-DOS is the most popular program currently calling itself a DOS. CP/M was the most popular prior to MS-DOS.
download
To download a file is to copy it from a remote computer to your own. The opposite is upload.
driver
A driver is a piece of software that works with the OS to control a particular piece of hardware, like a printer, scanner or mouse.
DRM
DRM can stand for either Digital Rights Management or Digital Restrictions Management. In either case, DRM is used to place restrictions upon the usage of digital media ranging from software to music to video.
DTML
The Document Template Mark-up Language is a subset of SGML and a superset of HTML used for creating documents that dynamically adapt to external conditions using its own custom tags and a little bit of Python. Note that it is quite different from the similarly named DHTML.
EDBIC
The EDBIC character set is similar to (but less popular than) the ASCII character set in concept, but is significantly different in layout. It tends to be found only on old machines.
embedded
An embedded system is a computer that lives inside another device and acts as a component of that device. For example, cars have an embedded computer under the hood that helps regulate much of their day-to-day operation. An embedded file lives inside another and acts as a portion of that file. This is frequently seen with HTML files having embedded audio files; audio files often embedded in HTML include AU files, MIDI files, SID files, WAV files, AIFF files, and MOD files. Most browsers will ignore these files unless an appropriate plug-in is present.

emulator
An emulator is a program that allows one computer platform to mimic another for the purposes of running its software. Typically (but not always) running a program through an emulator will not be quite as pleasant an experience as running it on the real system.

environment
An environment (sometimes also called a runtime environment) is a collection of external variable items or parameters that a program can access when run. Information about the computer's hardware and the user can often be found in the environment.

extension
Filename extensions allow a grouping of different file types by putting a tag at the end of the name, such as .doc or .pdf.

FAQ
A frequently asked questions file attempts to provide answers for all commonly asked questions related to a given topic.

FireWire
An incredibly fast type of serial port that offers many of the best features of SCSI at a lower price. Faster than most types of parallel port, a single FireWire port is capable of chaining many devices without the need of a terminator. FireWire is similar in many respects to USB but is significantly faster and somewhat more expensive. It is heavily used for connecting audio/video devices to computers, but is also used for connecting storage devices like drives and other assorted devices like printers and scanners.

fixed width
As applied to a font, fixed width means that every character takes up the same amount of space. That is, an "i" will be just as wide as an "m" with empty space being used for padding. The opposite is variable width. The most common fixed width font is Courier.

flash
Flash memory is similar to RAM. It has one significant advantage: it does not lose its contents when power is lost; it has two main disadvantages: it is slower, and it eventually wears out. Flash memory is frequently found in PCMCIA cards.

font
In a simplistic sense, a font can be thought of as the physical description of a character set. While the character set will define what sets of bits map to what letters, numbers, and other symbols, the font will define what each letter, number, and other symbol looks like. Fonts can be either fixed width or variable width and independently, either bitmapped or vectored. The size of the large characters in a font is typically measured in points.

FORTRAN
FORTRAN stands for formula translation and is the oldest computer language in the world. Today languages like C and Java are more popular, but FORTRAN is still heavily used in military software. It is somewhat amusing to note that when FORTRAN was first released back in 1958 its advocates thought that it would mean the end of software bugs. In truth of course by making the creation of more complex software practical, computer languages have merely created new types of software bugs.

FreeBSD
A free variant of Berkeley UNIX available for Alpha and x86 based machines. It was not as popular as Linux.

freeware
Freeware is software that is available for free with no strings attached. The quality is often superb as the authors are also generally users.

FTP
The file transfer protocol is one of the most commonly used methods of copying files across the Internet. It has its origins on UNIX machines, but has been adapted to almost every type of

computer in existence and is built into many browsers. Most FTP programs have two modes of operation, ASCII, and binary. Transmitting an ASCII file via the ASCII mode of operation is more efficient and cleaner. Transmitting a binary file via the ASCII mode of operation will result in a broken binary file. Thus the FTP programs that do not support both modes of operation will typically only do the binary mode, as binary transfers are capable of transferring both kinds of data without corruption.

gateway
A gateway connects otherwise separate computer networks.

GHz & gigahertz
One gigahertz is equivalent to 1000 megahertz, or 1,000,000,000 hertz.

GNOME
The GNU network object model environment was a popular free window manager (and much more -- as its name touts, it is more of a desktop environment) that ran under X-Windows. It was a part of the GNU project.

GNU
GNU stands for GNU's not UNIX and is thus a recursive acronym (and unlike the animal name, the "G" here is pronounced). At any rate, the GNU project is an effort by the Free Software Foundation (FSF) to make all of the traditional UNIX utilities free for whoever wants them.

HP-UX
HP-UX is the version of UNIX designed by Hewlett-Packard to work with their PA-RISC and 68xx based machines.

HTML
The Hypertext Mark-up Language is the language currently most frequently used to express web pages. Every browser has the built-in ability to understand HTML. Some browsers can additionally understand Java and browse FTP areas. HTML is a proper subset of SGML.

http
The hypertext transfer protocol is the native protocol of browsers and is most typically used to transfer HTML formatted files. The secure version is called "https".

Hz & hertz
Hertz means cycles per second, and makes no assumptions about what is cycling. So, for example, if a fluorescent light flickers once per jiffy, it has a 60 Hz flicker. More typical for computers would be a program that runs once per jiffy and thus has a 60 Hz frequency, or larger units of hertz like kHz, MHz, GHz, or THz.

iCalendar
The iCalendar standard refers to the format used to store calendar type information (including events, to-do items, and journal entries) on the Internet. iCalendar data can be found on some World-Wide-Web pages or attached to e-mail messages.

icon
A small graphical display representing an object, action, or modifier of some sort.

Inform
A compiled, object-oriented language optimized for creating interactive fiction.

infrared communications
A device with an infrared port can communicate with other devices at a distance by beaming infrared light signals. Two incompatible protocols are used for infrared communications: IrDA and ASK. Many devices support both.

Instant Messenger
AOL's Instant Messenger was a means of chatting over the Internet in real-time. It allowed both open group discussions and private conversations. Instant Messenger used a different, proprietary protocol from the more standard IRC, and was not supported on as many platforms.

interactive fiction
Interactive fiction (often abbreviated "IF" or "I-F") is a form of literature unique to the computer. While the reader cannot influence the direction of a typical story, the reader plays a more active role in an interactive fiction story and completely controls its direction. Interactive fiction works come in all the sizes and genres available to standard fiction, and in fact are not always even fiction per se (interactive tutorials exist and are slowly becoming more common).

interpreted
If a program is interpreted, its actual human-readable source is read as it is run by the computer. This is generally a slower process than if the program being run has already been compiled.

Intranet
An intranet is a private network. There are many intranets scattered all over the world. Some are connected to the Internet via gateways.

IP
IP is the family of protocols that makes up the Internet.

IRC
Internet relay chat is a means of chatting over the Internet in real-time. It allows both open group discussions and private conversations.

IrDA
The Infrared Data Association (IrDA) is a voluntary organization of various manufacturers working together to ensure that the infrared communications between different computers, printers, digital cameras, remote controls, etc. are all compatible with each other regardless of brand. The term is also often used to designate an IrDA compliant infrared communications port on a device. Informally, a device able to communicate via IrDA compliant infrared is sometimes simply said to "have IrDA". There is also an earlier, incompatible, and usually slower type of infrared communications still in use called ASK.

IRI
An Internationalized Resource Identifier is just a URI with i18n.

IRIX
The variant of UNIX designed by Silicon Graphics, Inc. IRIX machines are known for their graphics capabilities and were initially optimized for multimedia applications.

ISDN
An integrated service digital network line can be simply looked at as a digital phone line. ISDN connections to the Internet can be four times faster than the fastest regular phone connection, and because it is a digital connection a modem is not needed. Any computer hooked up to ISDN will typically require other special equipment in lieu of the modem, however. Also, both phone companies and ISPs charge more for ISDN connections than regular modem connections.

ISP
An Internet service provider is a company that provides Internet support for other entities.

Java
A computer language designed to be both fairly lightweight and extremely portable. It is tightly bound to the web as it is the primary language for web applets. There has also been an OS based on Java for use on small hand-held, embedded, and network computers. It is called JavaOS. Java can be either interpreted or compiled. For web applet use it is almost always interpreted. While its interpreted form tends not to be very fast, its compiled form can often rival languages like C++ for speed. It is important to note however that speed is not Java's primary purpose -- raw speed is considered secondary to portabilty and ease of use.

JavaScript
JavaScript (in spite of its name) has nothing whatsoever to do with Java (in fact, it's arguably more like Newton Script than Java). JavaScript is an interpreted language built into a browser to

provide a relatively simple means of adding interactivity to web pages. It is only supported on a few different browsers, and tends not to work exactly the same on different versions. Thus its use on the Internet is somewhat restricted to fairly simple programs. On intranets where there are usually fewer browser versions in use, JavaScript has been used to implement much more complex and impressive programs.

jiffy

A jiffy is 1/60 of a second. Jiffies are to seconds as seconds are to minutes.

joystick

A joystick is a physical device typically used to control objects on a computer screen. It is frequently used for games and sometimes used in place of a mouse. Today, joysticks are used for gaming, robotics, medical research, virtual reality (VR), and industrial control systems.

JSON

The JSON is used for data interchange between programs, an area in which the ubiquitous XML is not too well-suited. JSON is lightweight and works extremely cleanly with languages including JavaScript, Python, Java, C++, and many others.

JSON-RPC

JSON-RPC is like XML-RPC but is significantly more lightweight since it uses JSON in lieu of XML.

kernel

The very heart of an OS is often called its kernel. It will usually (at minimum) provide some libraries that give programmers access to its various features.

kHz & kilohertz

One kilohertz is equivalent to 1000 hertz. Some older computers have clock speeds measured in kHz.

LDAP

The Lightweight Directory Access Protocol provides a means of sharing address book type of information across an intranet or even across the Internet. Note too that "address book type of information" here is pretty broad; it often includes not just human addresses, but machine addresses, printer configurations, and similar.

library

A selection of routines used by programmers to make computers do particular things.

lightweight

Something that is lightweight will not consume computer resources (such as RAM and disk space) too much and will thus run on less expensive computer systems.

Linux

One of the fastest, most robust, and powerful multitasking OS systems. Linux can be downloaded for free or be purchased for a small service charge. Linux is available for more hardware combinations than any other OS. Fast, reliable, stable, and inexpensive, Linux is popular with ISPs, software developers, and home hobbyists alike.

load

There are two popular meanings for load. The first means to fetch some data or a program from a disk and store it in memory. The second indicates the amount of work a component (especially a processor) is being made to do.

Logo

Logo is an interpreted language designed by Papert in 1966 to be a tool for helping people (especially kids) learn computer programming concepts. In addition to being used for that purpose, it is often used as a language for controlling mechanical robots and other similar devices. Logo interfaces even exist for building block / toy robot sets. Logo uses a special graphics cursor called "the turtle", and Logo is itself sometimes called "Turtle Graphics". Logo is quite portable but not particularly fast. Versions can be found on almost every computer platform in the world. Additionally, some other languages (notably some Pascal versions) provide Logo-like interfaces for graphics-intensive programming.

lossy

If a process is lossy, it means that a little quality is lost when it is performed. If a format is lossy, it means that putting data into that format (or possibly even manipulating it in that format) will cause some slight loss. Lossy processes and formats are typically used for performance or resource utilization reasons. The opposite of lossy is lossless.

Lua

Lua is a simple interpreted language. It is extremely portable, and free versions exist for most platforms.

Mac OS

Mac OS is the OS used on Macintosh computers. There are two distinctively different versions of it; everything prior to version 10 (sometimes called Mac OS Classic) and everything version 10 or later (called Mac OS X).

Mac OS Classic

The OS created by Apple and originally used by Macs is frequently (albeit slightly incorrectly) referred to as Mac OS Classic (officially Mac OS Classic is this original OS running under the modern Mac OS X in emulation. Mac OS combines the functionality of both an OS and a window manager and is often considered to be the easiest OS to use. It is partially multitasking but will still sometimes crash when dealing with a buggy program. It is probably the second most popular OS, next only to Windows 'XP (although it is quickly losing ground to Mac OS X) and has excellent driver support and boasts a fair selection of games. Mac OS will run on PowerPC and 68xx based machines.

Mac OS X

Mac OS X (originally called Rhapsody) is the industrial strength OS produced by Apple to run on both PowerPC and x86 systems (replacing what is often referred to as Mac OS Classic. Mac OS X is at its heart a variant of UNIX and possesses its underlying power (and the ability to run many of the traditional UNIX tools, including the GNU tools).

machine language

Machine language consists of the raw numbers that can be directly understood by a particular processor. Each processor's machine language will be different from other processors' machine language. Although called "machine language", it is not usually what people think of when talking about computer languages. Machine language dressed up with mnemonics to make it a bit more human-readable is called assembly language.

Macintosh

A Macintosh (or a Mac for short) is a computer system that has Mac OS for its OS. There are a few different companies that have produced Macs, but by far the largest is Apple. The oldest Macs are based on the 68xx processor; somewhat more recent Macs on the PowerPC processor, and current Macs on the x86 processor. The Macintosh was really the first general purpose computer to employ a GUI.

MacTel

An x86 based system running some flavor of Mac OS.

mainframe

A mainframe is any computer larger than a small piece of furniture. A modern mainframe is more powerful than a modern workstation, but more expensive and more difficult to maintain.

MathML

The Math Mark-up Language is a subset of XML used to represent mathematical formulae and equations. Typically it is found embedded within XHTML documents, although as of this writing not all popular browsers support it.

megahertz

A million cycles per second, abbreviated MHz. This is often used misleadingly to indicate processor speed, because while one might expect that a higher number would indicate a faster processor, that logic only holds true within a given type of processors as different types of processors are capable of doing different amounts of work within a cycle. For a current example, either a 200 MHz PowerPC or a 270 MHz SPARC will outperform a 300 MHz Pentium.

middleware
Software designed to sit in between an OS and applications. Common examples are Java and Tcl/Tk.

MIME
The multi-purpose Internet mail extensions specification describes a means of sending non-ASCII data (such as images, sounds, foreign symbols, etc.) through e-mail. It commonly utilizes bcode.

MMX
Multimedia extensions were built into some x86 CPUs to provide better performance for certain operations, most notably graphics and sound. It is similar to AltiVec on the PowerPC CPUs. Like AltiVec, it requires special software for full performance benefits to be realized.

MOB
A movable object is a graphical object that is manipulated separately from the background. These are seen all the time in computer games. When implemented in hardware, MOBs are sometimes called sprites.

Modula-2 & Modula-3
Modula-2 is a procedural language based on Pascal by its original author in around the 1977 1979 time period. Modula-3 is an intended successor that adds support for object-oriented constructs (among other things). Modula-2 can be either compiled or interpreted, while Modula-3 tends to be just a compiled language.

MOTD
A message **of** the day. Many computers (particularly more capable ones) are configured to display a MOTD when accessed remotely.

MS-DOS
The DOS produced by Microsoft. Early versions of it bear striking similarities to the earlier CP/M, but it utilizes simpler commands. It provides only a CLI, but either OS/2, Windows 3.1, Windows '95, Windows '98, Windows ME, or GEOS may be run on top of it to provide a GUI. It only runs on x86 based machines.

MS-Windows
MS-Windows is the name collectively given to several somewhat incompatible OSes all produced by Microsoft. The latest Windows update is Windows 11, version 23H2.

MUD
A multi-user dimension (also sometimes called multi-user dungeon, but in either case abbreviated to "MUD") is sort of a combination between the online chatting abilities provided by something like IRC and a role-playing game. A MUD built with object oriented principles in mind is called a "Multi-user dimension object-oriented", or MOO. Yet another variant is called a "multi-user shell", or MUSH. Still other variants are called multi-user role-playing environments (MURPE) and multi-user environments (MUSE). There are probably more. In all cases the differences will be mostly academic to the regular user, as the same software is used to connect to all of them. Software to connect to MUDs can be found for most platforms, and there are even Java based ones that can run from within a browser.

multitasking
Some OSes have built into them the ability to do several things at once. This is called multitasking, and has been in use since the late sixties / early seventies. Since this ability is built into the software, the overall system will be slower running two things at once than it will be running just one thing. A system may have more than one processor built into it though, and such a system will be capable of running multiple things at once with less of a performance hit.

nagware
Nagware is a variant of shareware that will frequently remind its users to register.

NetBSD
A free variant of Berkeley UNIX available for Alpha, x86, 68xx, PA-RISC, SPARC, PowerPC, ARM, and many other types of machines. Its emphasis is on portability.
newbie
A newbie is a novice to the online world or computers in general.
news
Usenet news can generally be thought of as public e-mail as that is generally the way it behaves. In reality, it is implemented by different software and is often accessed by different programs. Different newsgroups adhere to different topics, and some are "moderated", meaning that humans will try to manually remove off-topic posts, especially spam. Most established newsgroups have a FAQ, and people are strongly encouraged to read the FAQ prior to posting.
Newton
Although Newton is officially the name of the lightweight OS developed by Apple to run on its MessagePad line of PDAs, it is often used to mean the MessagePads (and compatible PDAs) themselves and thus the term "Newton OS" is often used for clarity. The Newton OS is remarkably powerful; it is fully multitasking in spite of the fact that it was designed for small machines. It is optimized for hand-held use, but will readily transfer data to all manner of desktop machines. Historically it was the first PDA. Recently Apple announced that it will discontinue further development of the Newton platform, but will instead work to base future hand-held devices on either Mac OS or Mac OS X with some effort dedicated to making the new devices capable of running current Newton programs.
Newton book
Newton books provide all the functionality of ordinary books but add searching and hypertext capabilities. The format was invented for the Newton to provide a means of making volumes of data portable, and is particularly popular in the medical community as most medical references are available as Newton books and carrying around a one pound Newton is preferable to carrying around twenty pounds of books, especially when it comes to looking up something. In addition to medical books, numerous references, most of the classics, and many contemporary works of fiction are available as Newton books. Most fiction is available for free, most references cost money. Newton books are somewhat more capable than the similar Palm DOC; both are specific types of e-books.
nybble
A nybble is half a byte, or four bits. It is a case of computer whimsy; it only stands to reason that a small byte should be called a nybble. Some authors spell it with an "i" instead of the "y", but the "y" is the original form.
object-oriented
The term "object-oriented" applies to a philosophy of software creation. Often this philosophy is referred to as object-oriented design (sometimes abbreviated as OOD), and programs written with it in mind are referred to as object-oriented programs (often abbreviated OOP). Programming languages designed to help facilitate it are called object-oriented languages (sometimes abbreviated as OOL) and databases built with it in mind are called object-oriented databases (sometimes abbreviated as OODB or less fortunately OOD). The general notion is that an object-oriented approach to creating software starts with modeling the real-world problems trying to be solved in familiar real-world ways, and carries the analogy all the way down to structure of the program. This is of course a great over-simplification. Numerous object-oriented programming languages exist including: Java, C++, Modula-2, Newton Script, and ADA.
Objective-C & ObjC
Objective-C (often called "ObjC" for short) is a compiled object-oriented language. Based heavily on C, Objective-C is nearly as fast and can often be thought of as being just C with added features. Note that it was developed independently of C++; its object-oriented extensions are more in the style of Smalltalk. It is however related to Objective-C++.
Objective-C++ & ObjC++

Objective-C++ (often called "ObjC++" for short) is a curious hybrid of Objective-C and C++, allowing the syntax of both to coexist in the same source files.

office suite

An office suite is a collection of programs including at minimum a word processor, spreadsheet, drawing program, and minimal database program. Some popular office suites include Google Workspace, Microsoft 365, iWork, LibreOffice, Polaris Office and OpenOffice.

open source

Open source software goes one step beyond freeware. Not only does it provide the software for free, it provides the original source code used to create the software. Thus, curious users can poke around with it to see how it works, and advanced users can modify it to make it work better for them. By its nature, open source software is pretty well immune to all types of computer virus.

OpenBSD

A free variant of Berkeley UNIX available for Alpha, x86, 68xx, PA-RISC, SPARC, and PowerPC based machines. Its emphasis is on security.

OpenDocument & ODF

OpenDocument (or ODF for short) is the suite of open, XML-based office suite application formats defined by the OASIS consortium. It defines a platform-neutral, non-proprietary way of storing documents.

OpenGL

A low-level 3D graphics library with an emphasis on speed developed by SGI.

OS/2

OS/2 is the OS designed by IBM to run on x86 based machines. It is semi-compatible with MS-Windows. IBM's more industrial strength OS is called AIX.

Palm Pilot

The Palm Pilot (also called both just Palm and just Pilot, officially now just Palm) was the most popular PDA in use. It was one of the least capable PDAs but also one of the smallest and least expensive. While not as full-featured as many of the other PDAs (such as the Newton), it performed what features it did have quite well.

parallel

Loosely speaking, parallel implies a situation where multiple things can be done simultaneously, like having multiple check-out lines each serving people all at once. Parallel connections are by their nature more expensive than serial ones, but usually faster. Also, in a related use of the word, often multitasking computers are said to be capable of running multiple programs in parallel.

partition

Sometimes due to hardware limitations, disks have to be divided into smaller pieces. These pieces are called partitions.

Pascal

Named after the mathematician Blaise Pascal, Pascal is a language designed by Niklaus Wirth originally in 1968 (and heavily revised in 1972) mostly for purposes of education and training people how to write computer programs. It is a typically compiled language but is still usually slower than C or FORTRAN. Wirth also created a more powerful object-oriented Pascal-like language called Modula-2.

PC-DOS

The DOS produced by IBM designed to work like MS-DOS. Early versions of it bear striking similarities to the earlier CP/M, but it utilizes simpler commands. It provides only a CLI, but either Windows 3.1 or GEOS may be run on top of it to provide a GUI. It only runs on x86 based machines.

PCMCIA

The Personal Computer Memory Card International Association is a standards body that concern themselves with PC Card technology. Often the PC Cards themselves are referred

to as "PCMCIA cards". Frequently flash memory can be found in PC card form.
Perl
Perl is an interpreted language extremely popular for web applications.
PET
The Commodore PET (Personal Electronic Transactor) is an early (circa 1977-1980, around the same time as the Apple][) home computer featuring a ROM-based BASIC developed by Microsoft which it uses as a default "OS". It is based on the 65xx family of processors and is the precursor to the VIC-20.
PHP
Named with a recursive acronym (PHP: Hypertext Preprocessor), PHP provides a means of creating web pages that dynamically modify themselves on the fly.
ping
Ping is a protocol designed to check across a network to see if a particular computer is "alive" or not. Computers that recognize the ping will report back their status. Computers that are down will not report back anything at all.
pixel
The smallest distinct point on a computer display is called a pixel.
plug-in
A plug-in is a piece of software designed not to run on its own but rather work in cooperation with a separate application to increase that application's abilities.
point
There are two common meanings for this word. The first is in the geometric sense; a position in space without size. Of course as applied to computers it must take up some space in practice (even if not in theory) and it is thus sometimes synonymous with pixel. The other meaning is related most typically to fonts and regards size. The exact meaning of it in this sense will unfortunately vary somewhat from person to person, but will often mean 1/72 of an inch. Even when it does not exactly mean 1/72 of an inch, larger point sizes always indicate larger fonts.
PowerPC
The PowerPC is a RISC processor developed in a collaborative effort between IBM, Apple, and Motorola. It is currently produced by a few different companies, of course including its original developers. A few different OSes run on PowerPC based machines, including Mac OS, AIX, Solaris, Windows NT, Linux, Mac OS X, BeOS, and AmigaOS. At any given time, the fastest processor in the world is usually either a PowerPC or an Alpha, but sometimes SPARCs and PA-RISCs make the list, too.
proprietary
This simply means to be supplied by only one vendor. It is commonly misused. Currently, most processors are non-proprietary, some systems are non-proprietary, and every OS (except for arguably Linux) is proprietary.
protocol
A protocol is a means of communication used between computers. As long as both computers recognize the same protocol, they can communicate without too much difficulty over the same network or even via a simple direct modem connection regardless whether or not they are themselves of the same type. This means that WinTel boxes, Macs, Amigas, UNIX machines, etc., can all talk with one another provided they agree on a common protocol first.
queue
A queue is a waiting list of things to be processed. Many computers provide printing queues, for example. If something is being printed and the user requests that another item be printed, the second item will sit in the printer queue until the first item finishes printing at which point it will be removed from the queue and get printed itself.
RAM
Random access memory is the short-term memory of a computer. Any information stored in

RAM will be lost if power goes out, but the computer can read from RAM far more quickly than from a drive.
random access
Also called "dynamic access" this indicates that data can be selected without having to skip over earlier data first. This is the way that a CD, record, laserdisc, or DVD will behave -- it is easy to selectively play a particular track without having to fast forward through earlier tracks. The other common behavior is called sequential access.
RDF
The Resource Description Framework is built upon an XML base and provides a more modern means of accessing data from Internet resources. It can provide metadata (including annotations) for web pages making (among other things) searching more capable. It is also being used to refashion some existing formats like RSS and iCalendar; in the former case it is already in place (at least for newer RSS versions), but it is still experimental in the latter case.
real-time
Something that happens in real-time will keep up with the events around it and never give any sort of "please wait" message.
Rexx
The Restructured Extended Executor is an interpreted language designed primarily to be embedded in other applications in order to make them consistently programmable, but also to be easy to learn and understand.
RISC
Reduced instruction set computing is one of the two main types of processor design in use today, the other being CISC. The fastest processors in the world today are all RISC designs. There are several popular RISC processors, including Alphas, ARMs, PA-RISCs, PowerPCs, and SPARCs.
robot
A robot (or 'bot for short) in the computer sense is a program designed to automate some task, often just sending messages or collecting information. A spider is a type of robot designed to traverse the web performing some task (usually collecting data).
robust
The adjective robust is used to describe programs that are better designed, have fewer bugs, and are less likely to crash.
ROM
Read-only memory is similar to RAM only cannot be altered and does not lose its contents when power is removed.
RSS
RSS stands for either Rich Site Summary, Really Simple Syndication, or **RDF** Site Summary, depending upon whom you ask. The general idea is that it can provide brief summaries of articles that appear in full on a web site. It is well-formed XML, and newer versions are even more specifically well-formed RDF.
Ruby
Ruby is an interpreted, object-oriented language. Ruby was fairly heavily influenced by Perl, so people familiar with that language can typically transition to Ruby easily.
scanner
A scanner is a piece of hardware that will examine a picture and produce a computer file that represents what it sees. A digital camera is a related device. Each has its own limitations.
script
A script is a series of OS commands. The term "batch file" means much the same thing, but is a bit dated. Typically the same sort of situations in which one would say DOS instead of OS, it would also be appropriate to say batch file instead of script. Scripts can be run like programs, but tend to perform simpler tasks. When a script is run, it is always interpreted.

SCSI
Loosely speaking, a disk format sometimes used by MS-Windows, Mac OS, AmigaOS, and (almost always) UNIX. Generally SCSI is superior (but more expensive) to IDE, but it varies somewhat with system load and the individual SCSI and IDE components themselves. The quick rundown is that: SCSI-I and SCSI-II will almost always outperform IDE; EIDE will almost always outperform SCSI-I and SCSI-II; SCSI-III and UltraSCSI will almost always outperform EIDE; and heavy system loads give an advantage to SCSI. Note that although loosely speaking it is just a format difference, it is deep down a hardware difference.

sequential access
This indicates that data cannot be selected without having to skip over earlier data first. This is the way that a cassette or video tape will behave. The other common behavior is called random access.

serial
Loosely speaking, serial implies something that has to be done linearly, one at a time, like people being served in a single check-out line. Serial connections are by their nature less expensive than parallel connections (including things like SCSI) but are typically slower.

server
A server is a computer designed to provide various services for an entire network. It is typically either a workstation or a mainframe because it will usually be expected to handle far greater loads than ordinary desktop systems. The load placed on servers also necessitates that they utilize robust OSes, as a crash on a system that is currently being used by many people is far worse than a crash on a system that is only being used by one person.

SGML
The Standard Generalized Mark-up Language provides an extremely generalized level of mark-up. More common mark-up languages like HTML and XML are actually just popular subsets of SGML.

shareware
Shareware is software made for profit that allows a trial period before purchase. Typically shareware can be freely downloaded, used for a period of weeks (or sometimes even months), and either purchased or discarded after it has been learned whether or not it will satisfy the user's needs.

shell
A CLI designed to simplify complex OS commands. Some OSes (like AmigaOS, the Hurd, and UNIX) have built-in support to make the concurrent use of multiple shells easy. Common shells include the Korn Shell (ksh), the Bourne Shell (sh or bsh), the Bourne-Again Shell, (bash or bsh), the C-Shell (csh), etc.

SIMM
A physical component used to add RAM to a computer. Similar to, but incompatible with, DIMMs.

Smalltalk
Smalltalk is an efficient language for writing computer programs. Historically it is one of the first object-oriented languages, and is not only used today in its pure form but shows its influence in other languages like Objective-C.

spam
Generally spam is unwanted, unrequested e-mail or some other form of contact. It is typically sent out in bulk to huge address lists that were automatically generated by various robots endlessly searching the Internet and newsgroups for things that resemble e-mail addresses.

SPARC
The SPARC was a RISC processor developed by Sun.

sprite
The term sprite originally referred to a small MOB, usually implemented in hardware. Lately it

is also being used to refer to a single image used piecemeal within a Web site in order to avoid incurring the time penalty of downloading multiple files.

SQL

SQL (pronounced Sequel) is an interpreted language specially designed for database access. It is supported by virtually every major modern database system.

SVG

Scalable Vector Graphics data is an XML file that is used to hold graphical data that can be resized without loss of quality. SVG data can be kept in its own file, or even embedded within a web page (although not all browsers are capable of displaying such data).

Tonic

The Tool Command Language is a portable interpreted computer language designed to be easy to use. Tk is a GUI toolkit for Tcl. Tcl is a fairly popular language for both integrating existing applications and for creating Web applets (note that applets written in Tcl are often called Tcklets). Tcl/Tk is available for free for most platforms, and plug-ins are available to enable many browsers to play Tcklets.

TCP/IP

TCP/IP is a protocol for computer networks. The Internet is largely built on top of TCP/IP (it is the more reliable of the two primary Internet Protocols -- TCP stands for Transmission Control Protocol).

terminator

A terminator is a dedicated device used to mark the end of a device chain (as is most typically found with SCSI devices). If such a chain is not properly terminated, weird results can occur.

TEX

TEX (pronounced "tek") is a freely available, industrial strength typesetting program that can be run on many different platforms. These qualities make it exceptionally popular in schools, and frequently software developed at a university will have its documentation in TEX format. TEX is not limited to educational use, though; many professional books were typeset with TEX. TEX's primary drawback is that it can be quite difficult to set up initially.

THz & terahertz

One terahertz is equivalent to 1000 gigahertz.

TrackBack

TrackBacks essentially provide a means whereby different web sites can post messages to one another not just to inform each other about citations, but also to alert one another of related resources. Typically, a blog may display quotations from another blog through the use of TrackBacks.

UDP/IP

UDP/IP is a protocol for computer networks. It is the faster of the two primary Internet Protocols. UDP stands for User Datagram Protocol.

Unicode

The Unicode character set is a superset of the ASCII character set with provisions made for handling international symbols and characters from other languages. Unicode is sixteen bit, so takes up roughly twice the space as simple ASCII, but is correspondingly more flexible.

UNIX

UNIX is a family of OSes, each being made by a different company or organization but all offering a very similar look and feel. It cannot quite be considered non-proprietary, however, as the differences between different vendor's versions can be significant (it is still generally possible to switch from one vendor's UNIX to another without too much effort; today the differences between different UNIXes are similar to the differences between the different MS-Windows; historically there were two different UNIX camps, Berkeley / BSD and AT&T / System V, but the assorted vendors have worked together to minimize the differences). The free variant Linux is one of the closest things to a current, non-proprietary OS; its development is controlled by a non-profit organization and its distribution is provided by several companies. UNIX is powerful; it is fully multitasking and can do pretty much anything that any OS can do (look to the Hurd if you need a more powerful OS). With power comes complexity, however, and UNIX tends not to be overly friendly to beginners (although those who think UNIX is difficult or cryptic apparently have not used CP/M). Window managers are available for UNIX (running under X-Windows) and once properly configured common operations will be almost as simple on a UNIX machine as on a Mac. Out of all the OSes in current use, UNIX has the greatest range of hardware support. It will run on machines built around many different processors.

upload
To upload a file is to copy it from your computer to a remote computer. The opposite is download.

UPS
An uninterrupted power supply uses heavy duty batteries to help smooth out its input power source.

URI
A Uniform Resource Identifier is basically just a unique address for almost any type of resource. It is similar to but more general than a URL; in fact, it may also be a URN.

URL
A Uniform Resource Locator is basically just an address for a file that can be given to a browser. It starts with a protocol type (such as http, ftp, or gopher) and is followed by a colon, machine name, and file name in UNIX style. Optionally an octothorpe character "#" and and arguments will follow the file name; this can be used to further define position within a page and perform a few other tricks. Similar to but less general than a URI.

URN
A Uniform Resource Name is basically just a unique address for almost any type of resource unlike a URL it will probably not resolve with a browser.

USB
A really fast type of serial port that offers many of the best features of SCSI without the price. Faster than many types of parallel port, a single USB port is capable of chaining many devices without the need of a terminator. USB is much slower (but somewhat less expensive) than FireWire.

uucode
The point of uucode is to allow 8-bit binary data to be transferred through the more common 7-bit ASCII channels (most especially e-mail). The facilities for dealing with uucoded files exist for many different machine types, and the most common programs are called "uuencode" for encoding the original binary file into a 7-bit file and "uudecode" for restoring the original binary file from the encoded one. Sometimes different uuencode and uudecode programs will work in subtly different manners causing annoying compatibility problems. Bcode was invented to provide the same service as uucode but to maintain a tighter standard.

variable width
As applied to a font, variable width means that different characters will have different widths as appropriate. For example, an "i" will take up much less space than an "m". The opposite of variable width is fixed width. The terms "proportional width" and "proportionally spaced" mean the same thing as variable width. Some common variable width fonts include Times, Helvetica, and Bookman.

vector
This term has two common meanings. The first is in the geometric sense: a vector defines a direction and magnitude. The second concerns the formatting of fonts and images. If a font is a vector font or an image is a vector image, it is defined as lines of relative size and direction rather than as collections of pixels (the method used in bitmapped fonts and images). This makes it easier to change the size of the font or image, but puts a bigger load on the device that has to display the font or image. The term "outline font" means the same thing as vector font.

VIC-20
The Commodore VIC-20 computer sold millions of units and is generally considered to have been the first affordable home computer. It features a ROM-based BASIC and uses it as a default "OS". It is based on the 65xx family of processors. VIC (in case you are wondering) can stand for either video interface c or video interface computer. The VIC-20 is the precursor to the C64/128.

virtual machine
A virtual machine is a machine completely defined and implemented in software rather than hardware. It is often referred to as a "runtime environment"; code compiled for such a machine is typically called bytecode.

virtual memory
This is a scheme by which disk space is made to substitute for the more expensive RAM space. Using it will often enable a comptuer to do things it could not do without it, but it will also often result in an overall slowing down of the system. The concept of swap space is very similar.

virtual reality
Virtual reality (often called VR for short) is generally speaking an attempt to provide more natural, human interfaces to software. It can be as simple as a pseudo 3D interface or as elaborate as an isolated room in which the computer can control the user's senses of vision, hearing, and even smell and touch.

virus
A virus is a program that will seek to duplicate itself in memory and on disks, but in a subtle way that will not immediately be noticed. A computer on the same network as an infected computer or that uses an infected disk (even a floppy) or that downloads and runs an infected program can itself become infected. A virus can only spread to computers of the same platform. For example, on a network consisting of a WinTel box, a Mac, and a Linux box, if one machine acquires a virus the other two will probably still be safe.

VMS
The industrial strength OS that runs on VAXen.

VoIP
VoIP means "Voice over IP" and it is quite simply a way of utilizing the Internet (or even in some cases intranets) for telephone conversations. The primary motivations for doing so are cost and convenience as VoIP is significantly less expensive than typical telephone long distance packages, plus one high speed Internet connection can serve for multiple phone lines.

VRML
A Virtual Reality Modeling Language file is used to represent VR objects. It has essentially been superceded by X3D.

W3C
The World Wide Web Consortium (usually abbreviated W3C) is a non-profit, advisory body that makes suggestions on the future direction of the World Wide Web, HTML, CSS, and browsers.

Waba
An extremely lightweight subset of Java optimized for use on PDAs.

WebDAV
WebDAV stands for Web-based Distributed Authoring and Versioning, and is designed to provide a way of editing Web-based resources in place. It serves as a more modern (and often more secure) replacement for FTP in many cases.

WebTV
A1NebTV box hooks up to an ordinary television set and displays web pages. It will not display them as well as a dedicated computer.

window manager
A window manager is a program that acts as a graphical go-between for a user and an OS. It provides a GUI for the OS. Some OSes incorporate the window manager into their own internal code, but many do not for reasons of efficiency. Some OSes partially make the division. Some

common true window managers include CDE (Common Desktop Environment), GNOME, KDE, Aqua, OpenWindows, Motif, FVWM, Sugar, and Enlightenment. Some common hybrid window managers with OS extensions include Windows ME, Windows 98, Windows 95, Windows 3.1, OS/2 and GEOS.

WinTel
An x86 based system running some flavor of MS-Windows.

workstation
Depending upon whom you ask, a workstation is either an industrial strength desktop computer or its own category above the desktops. Workstations typically have some flavor of UNIX for their OS, but there has been a recent trend to call high-end Windows NT and Windows 2000 machines workstations, too.

WYSIWYG
What you see is what you get; an adjective applied to a program that attempts to exactly represent printed output on the screen. Related to WYSIWYM but quite different.

WYSIWYM
What you see is what you mean; an adjective applied to a program that does not attempt to exactly represent printed output on the screen, but rather defines how things are used and so will adapt to different paper sizes, etc. Related to WYSIWYG but quite different.

X-Face
X-Faces are small monochrome images embedded in headers for both provides a e-mail and news messages. Better mail and news applications will display them (sometimes automatically, sometimes only per request).

X-Windows
X-Windows provides a GUI for most UNIX systems, but can also be found as an add-on library for other computers. Numerous window managers run on top of it. It is often just called "X".

X3D
Extensible **3D** Graphics data is an XML file that is used to hold three-dimensional graphical data. It is the successor to VRML.

x86
The x86 series of processors includes the Pentium, Pentium Pro, Pentium II, Pentium III, Celeron, and Athlon as well as the 786, 686, 586, 486, 386, 286, 8086, 8088, etc. It is an exceptionally popular design (by far the most popular CISC series) in spite of the fact that even its fastest model is significantly slower than the assorted RISC processors. Many different OSes run on machines built around x86 processors, including MS-DOS, Windows 3.1, Windows '95, Windows '98, Windows ME, Windows NT, Windows 2000, Windows CE, Windows XP, GEOS, Linux, Solaris, OpenBSD, NetBSD, FreeBSD, Mac OS X, OS/2, BeOS, CP/M, etc. A couple different companies produce x86 processors, but the bulk of them are produced by Intel. It is expected that this processor will eventually be completely replaced by the Merced, but the Merced development schedule is somewhat behind. Also, it should be noted that the Pentium III processor has stirred some controversy by including a "fingerprint" that will enable individual computer usage of web pages etc. to be accurately tracked.

XBL
An XML Binding Language document is used to associate executable content with an XML tag. It is itself an XML file, and is used most frequently (although not exclusively) in conjunction with XUL.

XHTML
The Extensible Hypertext Mark-up Language is essentially a cleaner, stricter version of HTML. It is a proper subset of XML.

XML
The Extensible Mark-up Language is a subset of SGML and a superset of XHTML. It is used for numerous things including (among many others) RSS and RDF.

XML-RPC
XML-RPC provides a fairly lightweight means by which one computer can execute a program on a co-operating machine across a network like the Internet. It is based on XML and is used for everything from fetching stock quotes to checking weather forcasts.

XO
The energy-efficient, kid-friendly laptop produced by the OLPC project. It runs Sugar for its window manager and Linux for its OS. It sports numerous built-in features like wireless networking, a video camera & microphone, a few USB ports, and audio in/out jacks. It comes with several educational applications (which it refers to as "Activities"), most of which are written in Python.

XSL
The Extensible Stylesheet Language is like CSS for XML. It provides a means of describing how an XML resource should be displayed.

XSLT
XSL Transformations are used to transform one type of XML into another. It is a component of XSL that can be (and often is) used independently.

XUL
An XML User-Interface Language document is used to define a user interface for an application using XML to specify the individual controls as well as the overall layout.

Z-Machine
A virtual machine optimized for running interactive fiction, interactive tutorials, and other interactive things of a primarily textual nature. Z-Machines have been ported to almost every platform in use today. Z-machine bytecode is usually called Z-code. The Glulx virtual machine is of the same idea but somewhat more modern in concept.

zip
There are three common zips in the computer world that are completely different from one another. One is a type of removable removable disk slightly larger (physically) and vastly larger (capacity) than a floppy. The second is a group of programs used for running interactive fiction. The third is a group of programs used for compression.

www.ingramcontent.com/pod-product-compliance
Lightning Source LLC
Chambersburg PA
CBHW082039300426
44117CB00015B/2539